25 Contemporary Issues in Law Enforcement

Including a Scenario Driven Assignment Guide

Kimberly Karlberg
Joliet Junior College

Kendall Hunt
publishing company

Kendall Hunt
publishing company

www.kendallhunt.com
Send all inquiries to:
4050 Westmark Drive
Dubuque, IA 52004-1840

Printed in the United States of America
10 9 8 7 6 5 4 3 2 1

A day in the life of an officer can be a wind-tunnel experience. All in all, we are only human. Learn by these scenarios. Recognize contemporary issues, which will begin the healing process associated with the negative perception of law enforcement that continues to loom large in American society. Remember: Safety always comes first. Never jeopardize your safety. Believe in what you do, for you do it for society. If they do not seem appreciative, remind yourself that without you, a cruel world could surface. Do not allow your emotions to steer you; allow reason, good sense, ethics, and human understanding to be your guide. Never fall prey to lack of communication and be vigilent of your surroundings, for you could lose your life in an instant. Always cater to reaction, and in tense situations, grasp the art of communication. If all these factors are recognized, a successful law enforcement officer will be created.

Karlberg, 2012

Contents

Inductive logic

Empirical data was collected, and a generalization has been developed that explains relationships between/among the subjects observed. At certain times when interacting with individuals, why is a nonthreatening approach more productive than traditional policing approaches?

Comstock

"Case Closed"

The September 11, 2006 issue of *People* Magazine debuted the story of detective Cheryl Comstock of the Los Angeles County Sheriff's Department, Homicide Division. "How do you catch a killer 20 years after his crime? Cheryl Comstock did it by being extra nice. Not long ago she paid a visit to Arturo J. Gutierrez, once a suspect in a late '80s murder case that had gone ice cold. 'He had a dog,' says Comstock, 'I asked him to hold my folder while I petted the dog.' She also asked if he remembered when he'd last seen girlfriend, Christie Fleming, before she was found bludgeoned to death in her apartment in 1989. 'He said multiple times that he hadn't seen her in months,' says Comstock. 'We just kept going over his story in a nonthreatening way.' Then she politely thanked him for his time and left."

> Law enforcement officials and society have one common goal: to thwart crime and/or interfere with its plans.

Acknowledgments

I would like to acknowledge all the individuals who supported my writing of this textbook. First and foremost, I would like to acknowledge my family, Jeff and Lexy, and friends who on a regular basis inspired me to complete these writings. My mother-in-law, Dolores T. Karlberg, who continuously inspired my writings and insisted on the publication of this text. In addition, I would like to acknowledge my Aunt Mary Peikert, for her wise and uplifting advice.

Several colleagues commented on this book. I am grateful to them for their insight. I would like to recognize my editor JES. I'd also like to recognize Edward Senu Oke from the Social and Behavioral Science Department at Joliet Junior College, Joliet, Illinois, who inspired both my work as a writer and professor and who once told me to stay on *the right side of the road*, which I have continued to do. In addition, I thank him for writing the foreword to this manuscript.

I'd like to thank Jay Whitney for direction pertaining to this text. I'd like to acknowledge Gad Bensinger Ph.D., a professor in the Criminal Justice Department at Loyola University, Chicago, for teaching me the right way during the completion of my undergraduate and graduate degrees. I would like to recognize Robert Brown, Ph.D., Westwood College in Woodridge, Illinois for always supporting me as a professor of Criminal Justice. I would like to thank Commander Samuel Cannerday from the Berwyn, Illinois Police Department, who was my first instructor and one who guided my career in an ironic fashion. I would like to recognize Mike Casali (FIC), Bureau of Alcohol, Tobacco and Firearms, for believing in me and my abilities at the federal level; and senior special agent Dale Lange of Burlington Northern Santa Fe Police Department in Chicago for believing in my tactical policing abilities. I cannot forget Brendan Caffrey, the best supervisor I have ever had, for his belief in my ability in the private sector.

This text is for all of my students at Joliet Junior College, Joliet, Illinois; Westwood College, including the Woodridge Campus, Illinois; Schiller Park Campus, Illinois; and Calumet City Campus, Illinois for supporting my teachings and work in the Criminal Justice Field. I would like to thank all of my students globally attending Kaplan University Online, and formally Colorado Technical University online for their encouragement and support. I cannot forget

Eric Jankovic for all his encouragement. Additionally, I would like to thank my fellow law enforcement associates for guest-speaking in my classes and employing my philosophy when policing.

In Loving Memory of
Dolores T. Karlberg
March 18, 1934–March 27, 2006

Foreword

As a graduate of Eastern Kentucky University College of Law Enforcement and current chairperson of Joliet Junior College, Department of Social and Behavioral Sciences, I have had the opportunity to review many law enforcement textbooks and pertinent text materials, and I have found this textbook to be comprehensive. In the post–Rodney King era of uncertainty about the parameters of police powers, this textbook effectively speaks to the essentials of law enforcement training and the criminal justice system. The scenario-based approach of the text elucidates the practical basis of a practitioner's work in preparing students in law enforcement programs and criminal justice studies.

This textbook will be equally useful for students taking a course of study in criminalistics, as the text informs the psychological and sociological foundations for the study of behavioral sciences–related issues. The tenor of the text is indicative of the need for a more dynamic approach to the study of law enforcement, criminal justice, and the behavioral sciences. The text explicitly and implicitly shows that academic preparation should go beyond what is, into the realm of what every officer ought to know, and should know to meet changing demands. Parts I and II of the text focus on communication training and problem-solving attitudes that are essential in law enforcement officers' interaction with members of the public. The textbook shows that effective law enforcement officers must by necessity and training be well versed in using the least volatile methods of their training to diffuse tense situations. The textbook shows that officers who possess appropriate persuasive and communication skills are better equipped to temper the outward manifestation of human thoughts and emotions when assessing potential levels of dangerousness.

Parts III and IV of this textbook address the public engagement function of law enforcement, as a way of resensitizing law enforcement training and criminal justice studies to the efficacy of human relations functions. This textbook reflects on ways to gear the mind of the officer to the notion of power distribution, when engaged in fact finding and investigatory practices. Equally, the scenarios dealing with community policing and ethical dilemmas, such as abuse of power and corruption, bring to mind issues of negative public perception of the police and how public trust can be regained. These parts reinforce the fundamental imperative of training officers in the tenets of the Bill of Rights with emphasis on the Fourth Amendment guarantees for suspects and accused persons.

Part V informs the theoretical basis for attention to the adaptive and coping temperament that law enforcement officers need to imbibe, not only as professionals, but also as human beings who have relationships with significant others. The materials covered in Part V of the textbook are invaluable in the educational preparation of a balanced law enforcement officer, whose ethical responsibility is to protect the public interest, including balancing the pressures of home and work. The textbook brings to mind that all positive human attributions begin at the domestic front, and invariably, the scenario on partner communication speaks to why work-related stressors must not be allowed to interfere with home life. The textbook speaks to why law enforcement training must be wholesome, holistic, and never conducted in a vacuum. Most importantly, the textbook informs the theory that best practices in law enforcement training must be an inclusive enterprise, which highlights the importance of domestic relations and the good life of the officer's immediate family. I believe this textbook is a must read for every law enforcement officer, and for all students who plan to pursue a professional career in the field of law enforcement.

Edward O. Senu-Oke
Department of Social & Behavioral Sciences
Joliet Junior College, Joliet, Illinois

Part I

Communicational Training and the Lack Thereof

Concerning Power and Authoritarianism

Issue 1

"The idea of acting morally must extend to how a company treats its employees. Rather than focusing just on what they earn, you listen to what they need. You harness their energy and opinions. You empower them. The old authoritarian mode no longer works".

— Anita Roddick

Scenario 1: It Is All About the Power

> The only reason that I decided to become a police officer is because I wanted authority
> and power. My dad always thought that he was the king of the household and constantly
> picked on me. I guess I showed him. Now when I see my dad, he is scared of me because
> I can beat him down at any time. I wear my uniform all the time to prove to my dad and
> all my brothers who picked on me growing up that I now have the power over everyone
> and can do whatever I want without any consequences because I believe that I am above
> the law. I am a police officer.

Unfortunately power associated with law enforcement is implied. Some individuals who yearn for policing jobs have ulterior motives, because at some time in their life they have been a victim of an unfortunate circumstance. These motives create show-offs, using the badge as a power symbol rather than one of a public servant. An "anything goes" attitude, in order to prove power, does not correspond with that of a serve-and-protect agenda. An officer who accepts the goals of a public servant will remember that power concerns itself with the cost of resistance, and coercing effectively will not resort to one having to use power. An officer needs to be able to react to subjects through communication, forgetting about notions that power has been established because a firearm is being carried, a uniform is worn, and a badge is carried. A professional officer will always keep in mind that the job is to protect and serve, and that power/authoritarianism in most instances are rarely needed. Carl B. Klockars, in *Blue Lies and Police Placebos* (1984), examines truth in law enforcement. Klockars identifies four general types of control used by police officers: *authority, power, persuasion, force*. The use of persuasion should be at the forefront of policing. Eloquent persuasion, exemplified through the art of communication, can and should be used frequently. Close and Meier (1995) examine persuasion:

Rather, persuasion actively engages resistance and seeks to overcome it by mobilizing signs, symbols, words, and arguments that induce in the mind of the person persuaded the belief that he or she ought to comply. (p. 229)

Persuasion through active communication can lead to nonresistant arrests, willful convictions, and even complete compliance.

Scenario 2: I Must Show Off My Power in a Threatening Sort of Way

It was the Fourth of July, and for the first time in years, I was out partying all night. I decided to take public transportation so that I could enjoy myself and not worry about having to drive home. I was a bit obnoxious when approached by this nice police officer. We were having a calm conversation. Her tone of voice was soothing, and I no longer felt the need to continue my violent behavior. She listened to me and responded to what I had to say. Unfortunately, her supervisor walked up to us while we were speaking and decided to remind me of his power. He stated, "Hey what's going on? It is a good thing that you are talking to this officer because you know what happens when you talk to me?" I replied, "What?" The officer replied, "I'd take you to jail!" Subsequently, I felt threatened and reacted to this officer by telling him where to put it. I ended up in jail that night.

The form of discourse used by this supervisor was used to establish the idea that he was more powerful than the subject. However, this type of discourse did nothing more than enhance the subject's aggressive state of mind, present a challenge, and ultimately destroy the peaceful situation. Subsequently, the offender was taken into custody. This undesirable consequence could have been avoided by continuing practical discourse with the subject. However, when the supervisor decided to intervene and insinuate that he had more power than the subject, a challenge surfaced, and subsequently a combative subject surfaced.

The officer felt the need to establish power over the subject, but was it really necessary? Understanding a subject's state of mind is necessary as well as not catering to annoying triggers such as brandishing the idea that the officer has more power and authority. A professional officer would have not aggravated the situation with threatening discourse; instead, a continued pursuit of calming the individual with tactful discourse should have been noted, and thus a positive outcome would have been established. The power associated with law enforcement is also entwined with authoritarianism. "*I have power over you*" and/or "*I have authority over you*" seemingly are of one agenda. In fact, both have one common feature, and Close and Meier (1995) note the similarities:

Both are social as opposed to individual forms of dominance and control. They both depend upon persons acting in concert, sharing and coordinating meanings and actions. (p. 228)

Authoritarianism and power associated with law enforcement officials are social misconceptions that need to be rectified. Authority demands an unquestioning obedience. How can productive communication surface if an unquestioning obedience is immediately demanded? Power is concerned with the cost of resistance. *"If I resist, what will happen?"* Both can be practiced interchangeably and abused simultaneously. *"If you move, I will knock you out!"* An officer is demanding obedience, yet at the same time wielding power. Therefore, authoritarianism and power are subject to one agenda.

What is known, though, is that all three major movements in the history of American police, their militarization, their professionalism, and their legalization are easily readable as direct attempts to encourage authoritative relations between police and citizens. Despite the fact that all three movements have been successful in some respects, all of them have met a peculiarly American mix of individualism, egalitarianism, and social heterogeneity fundamentally hostile to the enlargement of relations of authority. (Close & Meier, 1995)

By using active communication skills, authoritarianism and/or power should surface as a last resort. Explaining and/or reasoning to obtain compliance will alleviate tension and, in essence, establish control for the officer over the situation, while eliminating a threat and a negative perception of the officer. Authoritarian behavior related to law enforcement is rarely needed. So why is it implied? Our country is based on equality. Officers need to enforce the law, but not in the manner of tyranny, because being a dictator is not a deterrent. In fact, it innately challenges the other individual. Furthermore, when officers are perceived as threats, that perception, which stems from an authoritarian, militant nature, means that "the game is on." The "game" is considered to be a challenge and challenges the subject. However, when an officer's communication style is viewed as nonthreating, then the challenge is invalidated and social order is maintained.

Scenario 3: Eliminating a Powerful Threat

A correctional lieutenant has seen it all in the Cook County Jail. The following incident is one in which a violent offender was brought to his division. This guy was bloody and would not stop fighting with everyone. In fact, he had been fighting all night with the officers who brought him into the jail. So he says to me, "When I get untied, I am going to really hurt you!" I said to him, "If that is the worst thing that happens to me today, then I will be doing good. Hey, I am just doing my job, buddy. I have a family, too." The suspect remained calm for the rest of the evening.

The officer in this scenario alleviated the threat of his presence, and subsequently the suspect remained calm for the rest of the evening. By the officer stating his job title and implying that if the offender did hurt him that pain would not be the worst experience of the evening, he allowed the offender to believe that the officer would not fight back and in essence was not a threat. The suspect, believing that the officer alleviated the threatening environment by saying he would not engage in violent conduct no longer felt the need to be defensive or obnoxious. Moreover, the officer's statement that he had a job to do allowed the offender to relate to the officer as an equal, a fellow human, and one who was simply trying to pay the bills. If the officer simply stated that he was just doing his job, did not ever feel like fighting, and continued to apply accommodating discourse, the offender would have remained calm. The more non-threatening discourse that an officer can apply, the less likely a situation is going to escalate.

However, if the officer had replied, *"Yeah? Why don't you try it buddy!"* then the offender would have become even more noxious, because a challenge would have been offered. Therefore, the officer would have left the suspect with no choice but to react to a provocation. A challenge becomes a game; a game takes two to play and relates to challenging discourse furthered by physical abuse, which ultimately reveals who is more powerful. When an officer gives into a suspect/offender's threatening behavior, then a game is established. If the officer did untie the individual and attempt to teach him a powerful lesson (not unlike many who have done so) by fighting the suspect to prove that he is and will always be the winner, then the officer has committed a crime of battery. An officer's worst-case scenario is that there are video cameras in the prison that catch the officer in the act. The tape reaches the media. The officer is suspended, possibly indefinitely. To pursue this thought further, a civil lawsuit could be filed by the suspect alleging injuries and mental anguish, and demanding punitive and compensatory damages from not only the officer, but the organization whom hired him. If an officer decides to give into a suspect/offender's threat and verbally or physically abuses the suspect/offender just to prove dominance/power, then that officer has committed a crime. Walker (1992) examines police brutality.

Public disrespect was typically greeted by police brutality, which went unpunished. Continued use of force by the police only encouraged more public hostility. Ultimately this vicious circle led to a complete lack of public respect for police officers and a lack of professionalism in American policing. (p.10)

An officer's job is to thwart violence and calm situations, not heighten them. Too many times officers get caught up in the moment, adrenalin kicks in, and a powerful surge of aggression is acted on. Therefore, we witness cops beating suspects, television shows highlighting this behavior, and overall media frenzy blaming the police for anything and everything. Communication is the key to successful outcomes. An officer should practice the art of communication, and not verbally or physically react to a suspect/offender's threatening discourse. One lapse of judgment or loss of control may cause a loss of employment and/or incarceration. Most importantly, when engaged in challenging situations, cater to discourse, and in turn, the public's perception of law enforcement will be enhanced.

Name: _____ Date: _____

Assignment Guide Issue 1: Concerning Power and Authoritarianism

Group discussion assignment

- In Scenario 2, what should the supervising officer have done differently?
- In Scenario 3, do you think this type approach will always work or just in some instances? Please cite examples to discuss with the class.

Don't Hesitate to Communicate, but Proceed with Caution

Issue 2

If citizens were asked what traits they felt were desirable in police officers, their responses might go something like this: "Police officers should be able to work under pressure, to accept direction, to express themselves orally and in writing. They should have self-respect and the ability to command respect from others. They should use good judgment; and they should be considerate, compassionate, dependable, enthusiastic, fair, flexible, honest, humble, industrious, intelligent, logical, motivated, neat, observant, physically fit, prompt, resourceful, self-assured, stable, tactful, warm, and willing to listen and accept change. Furthermore, with our society becoming increasingly diverse, the ideal officer would be able to police without bias or discrimination and be sensitive to the needs and concerns of various populations within a community." Unfortunately, no one has all of these traits, but the more of these traits that police officers have, the more likely they are to be effective in dealing with not only the citizens of the community, but law breakers as well. (Wrobleski & Hess 2003, p. 374)

Scenario 4: Yes, Speak! It Is Okay

There was one incident when I almost died. It was a typical loss prevention stop. At first I could not figure out how this individual was stealing. It took me quite a while to figure out her network; however, it finally hit me. I went up to the second level, where the individual exited the store. I identified myself; she looked at me as I was standing next to the upper level balcony. She continued to look at me, and then the railing to the balcony. We both knew what she was thinking. She was in position not to comply with my request to return to the store, but to throw me over the balcony. She was twice my size, and I was working alone. We paused for a long time before I realized that I should start talking. I managed to talk my way out of being launched over the balcony, but I knew that I had an even more challenging task to overcome when we arrived at the office. She was cold, angry, hateful, not remorseful, and very belligerent. I had never talked so much in my life. My goal was to allow her to see my side. Over an hour later, she spoke. Another hour later, she understood what I was doing, and as time continued to pass, I understood why she did what she did. She even shook my hand before leaving for lock-up. Several months later I received a letter from her stating that I had changed her life. I broke the bad cop stereotype. For me this was a great accomplishment. I owed it all to the art of communication, understanding, and simple human nature.

The officer in this scenario decided not to remain silent, but to apply nonthreatening discourse. Frequently, subjects are combative and use threatening discourse. An officer's freedom to communicate is restricted by administration and learned responses from academies that they have attended. Officers are conditioned not to react to subject communication. In fact, the "beat" teaches one to either ignore it and/or threaten the subject with traditional discourse, such as, "Shut up or you're going to jail"; "One more word and you're under arrest"; "I don't care, take it up with the courts." Dehumanizing discourse looms large, such as not speaking to the subject but speaking to another officer in front of the subject about the subject. Do not hesitate to ask questions to find out what is going on in the offender's life at the time of arrest. Offer help if needed, whether it is a telephone call, employment guidance, or educational direction. Do not be afraid to break the bad cop stereotype. By breaking it, you are changing the public's perception of law enforcement from a negative to a positive one. The more talking one can participate in, the better the outcome. These are human beings with real problems and poor direction. Communication will aid in breaking the poor perception of law enforcement officers.

We need to start over, restructuring the mindset of law enforcement officers to pursue a form of social engagement and thwart the characteristics of the authoritarian ideology currently in place. Muir (1977) writes:

The reality and the subtle irony of being a policeman is that while he may appear to be the supreme practitioner of coercion, in fact he is the first and foremost its most frequent victim ... Contrary to the more unflattering stereotypes of policeman, it is the citizen who virtually always initiates the coercive encounter. What is more, the citizen tends to enjoy certain inordinate advantages over the policeman in these transactions ... the citizen is relative to the policeman, the more disposed, the more detached the nastier, and the crazier ... The irony of the policeman's lot is that his authority, his status, his sense of civility, and his reasonableness impose terrible limits on his freedom to react to the extortionate practices of others. (Muir, 1977, 44–45)

Remove the limits.

Scenario 5: Observational Speech

> At the local level of policing, it was a party gone bad because of underage drinking. We must have arrested 30 underage drinkers. We brought them to the station and began telephoning parents to pick up their children. I was honored with babysitting these 30 juveniles until their parents arrived. I sat in the room and listened for a long time. I knew that there were cameras in the station, so I was very hesitant to communicate with these individuals. They began to ask me questions, but I ignored them for as long as possible. Fortunately, I took it upon myself to break the bad cop stereotype, and I began speaking, but as little as possible. I learned so much information from these juveniles. I learned about their drug and alcohol use, where the parties are normally held, and I even learned who had drug and/or alcohol addiction problems and needed help. Of course, at this time I did not act on any of the information for fear that I would lose my job. They left the station shouting lines like "You're a cool cop!" and "You understand!" and "If we ever get in trouble, can we call you?" The change in attitude that I witnessed was amazing; they went from being cop haters to asking me if they could give me a telephone number. It was a huge turnaround, all due to the art of communication. Interpersonal communication is key to success in this field.

The officer in this scenario was hesitant to speak, yet just a bit of communication led to information that was valuable. The more one communicates, the more likely one is to gain vital information. The officer obviously realized that the juveniles wanted to communicate, and the officer decided to talk with the juveniles regardless of administrative consequences.

Ultimately, a positive outcome was noted. When a professional officer makes an arrest, the suspect is asked why and how, and ultimately the truth is uncovered. While dealing with many individuals who are arrested at the local level of policing, an officer must learn how to remove the *bad cop* stigma through use of communication by simply asking questions, offering guidance, and stimulating discourse. Subsequently, a positive outcome will be noted. Reece and Brandt take note of communication breakdown (2002).

Communication breakdown has just about taken the place of original sin as an explanation for the ills of the world—and perhaps with good cause. As our world becomes more complex and we spend more time in organized activities, the need for interpersonal understanding has never been greater. And just as important, the cost of failure has never been higher. (p. 33)

Scenario 6: Filters, an Altered State of Perception

A call came in that four individuals were harassing passengers. Everyone heard the call, and three officers were waiting for the alleged offender's arrival inside the facility. Having been present, a 26-year-old African-American male and a 62-year-old white male veteran officer were also present. Age is important because it is a factor contributing to the changes in behavior from younger recruits to older veteran officers. The four white male suspects walked directly into the three officers. They were what society has coined skinheads with a subtitle leaning toward Sharps, but currently traditional. The seasoned officer immediately stereotyped the individuals and attacked them by threatening to remove them from the building and put them in jail. The veteran officer said, "Look at these freaks. Do you want to go to jail? I will put you in jail right now!" The four alleged offenders became angry and abusive.

The appearance of these four individuals was different. They were wearing leather clothing and chains. Their hair color ranged from pink to blue. Their shoelaces were differently colored than their shoes, and several piercings were noted. The older police officer stated as they were walking toward him, *"Look at these freaks!"* Subsequently, he began verbally attacking the individuals. In an ideal situation, a professional officer would have immediately removed the stereotype and/or label and stated, *"What is the problem? What happened?"* The suspects then could explain that they had just missed their ride and were upset.

One officer could reply, *"Oh, I didn't know that you missed your ride. I thought you were angry at other individuals."* The suspects might reply, *"We were yelling at our ride because we were angry that we missed it. We can wait for another ride."*

Problem solved; the seasoned officer in the given scenario reacted to the appearance of the four suspects with an altered state of perception. Filters on approaching individuals based on appearance will definitely provoke controversy, and if acting on filtered perceptions, the end result will be a negative one. Alleviate any type of stereotypical thoughts. Furthermore, stereotyping and/or labeling alter one's perception and leads to prejudging, which filters the communication process. The seasoned officer first commented on the appearance of the individuals, assuming they had committed a crime. He screamed, *"You're all going to jail"* before he even knew what had occurred. Therefore, a communication barrier was established, which deterred productive communication—a devastating mistake made by many police officers who unnecessarily shotgun a situation based on one looking the part and subsequently, communication breakdown indicative of a filtered state of perception occurs. Unnecessary demands and talk are common, in turn provoking anger toward suspects, rather than an officer disregarding stereotypes and engaging in discourse to allow the root cause of a dilemma to surface and be corrected. Reece and Brandt (2002) examine communication filters:

When people are influenced by one or more of these filters, their perception of the message may be totally different from what the sender was attempting to communicate. Both sender and receiver must be keenly aware of these possible distortions so that they can intercept any miscommunication. (p. 33)

One officer asked the suspects about their appearance and what it meant. They replied that on a daily basis they are harassed by the police because of the way they look; however, they are just expressing themselves in a way that appeals to them. The subjects said that they did not like the seasoned officer's approach, that they were insulted, it made them angry, and they wanted to fight back. Another officer approached and also began asking questions.

What if an officer approached you and said, "What is your name? Do you have drugs on you?" They replied that his attitude was poor and, therefore, they argued with him about answering his questions. Furthermore, they asked him why almost the first question that came out of his mouth assumed they had drugs. What if an officer approached you and said, "Do you need any assistance? Can I help? What just happened?"

We spoke with these individuals for an hour. We learned about them, and they learned about us. We encouraged conversation and gained information from the subjects. "We decided to learn about the subjects rather than passing judgment based on their appearance. We learned that Skinheads and Sharps hate racial discrimination, and the only difference between them and us was simply music. There are many sender and receiver filters that interrupt communication and/or alter it." Do not fall prey to prejudice of any kind.

Scenario 7: I Misunderstood

I went to pick up my wife at work. She teaches college and had a late class. I arrived at the parking lot of the college and realized that I was several minutes early. I drove to the back of the parking lot and parked my car under a light because I wanted to read. An officer pulled up behind my vehicle and asked me what I was doing. I replied that I was waiting for my wife to get out of class. He then asked me why I don't go into the college and get my wife. I replied that I did not want to embarrass my wife. At that time he asked me to step out of the car and told me that he was going to search my car. Three other police vehicles arrived at the scene. I told him that he had no probable cause to search my vehicle. He then told me to immediately leave the parking lot. After class, my wife was greeted by this officer. He asked if I was her husband and reminded her of a drug charge that I had three years before I even met my wife. He explained to her that when I said that I would embarrass her, he thought I meant by causing a domestic dispute and was threatened by my appearance because I am 6 feet-1 inch and weigh 250 pounds. However, I meant that I was wearing shorts and a t-shirt and that I did not feel adequately dressed to enter the college.

The officer in this scenario assumed that the individual was threatening an act of domestic violence. A professional officer would have asked the subject to explain the statement, *"I will embarrass her,"* and the confusion would have been resolved.

Sender and Receiver Filters:

Role expectations

Attitudes

Emotions

Semantics

Language

Perception

Prejudice

Stereotypes (appearance)

Non-verbal gestures

Race/Gender

Labels

(Reece, Brandt, 1995)

Communication is easily taken for granted and thought of as a simple task. It assumes that a message can be understood with no need for explanation. Messages can be interpreted in different ways, and furthermore, one must realize that there are filters so that barriers become apparent. The communication process seems simple; however, recognition of sender and receiver filters that affect our communication process is needed. Learning how to become good listeners and how to make clarifying statements needs to be routinely practiced. The basic communication process involves a sender, then the message; subsequently the message is received, and feedback is awaited. There are filters that need to be avoided at any cost. Filters exist, and acknowledgment of these filters is significant. For example, if there is a language barrier, attempt to address the barrier. Filters can be devastating to communication because they can alter perception. A professional officer will block out perceptions based on appearance or perceptions. Remember the old saying, *Never judge a book by its cover.*

Scenario 8: I Knew She Would Cry

One of my worst experiences occurred when I was driving to the hospital. I was pregnant and highly emotional. I didn't feel well and was having pains in my lower abdomen. I saw flashing lights behind me. I had to pull over even though I needed to reach the hospital. The officer approached my vehicle. I attempted to tell him that I was sick, but he did not listen to me. By this time I felt faint and began to cry. He threw a ticket at me and stated, "Women are always crying!"

A favorite departmental story is one about a female who cries, and another is about a female who offers sexual favors in exchange for not being ticketed. Thwarting gender-specific stereotypes will not be an easy task. Society lives through stereotypes, labels, and discrimination. The media dictates how society should perceive other individuals. This officer obviously stereotyped and labeled the female driver. Subsequently, he expected a certain behavior. Therefore, a communication filter surfaced. Listening to the driver was not a priority. The driver could have needed an ambulance and a police escort to the hospital. When a subject seems disturbed, an officer has a duty to react to the disturbance, especially if illness of any sort is involved. Any filter can alter an officer's perception of the driver and subsequently interfere with proper judgment. Thus when a male officer pulls over a female driver, a gender filter could surface, predisposing the officer to a certain reaction. By not listening to the female driver, or maybe by listening too much, an altered state begins to take its course. Reece and Brandt (2002) reasonably identify a gender specific focus:

This filter makes it appear that men and women are communicating through different genderlects, just as people from different cultures use different dialects. This anger and frustration can create a major filter that interferes with effective communication between genders. (p. 37)

It is difficult to remove communication filters, including stereotypes and predispositions. However, this behavior passes false judgments on others, and innocent ones can indeed seem guilty in the eyes of the officer. The media dictates stereotypes and labels on television, radio, movies, and even now with use of internet. A professional officer will not employ predisposed judgments because it interferes with performance.

Scenario 9: He Was a Gangster

> When I attend my classes, I always attempt to look the part. A conservative look is demanded at the college level. I was on my way to class for my final presentation. My presentation was about human relations in a gang setting. My presentation involved looking the part and presenting my evidence, which was collected and videotaped in the real world. I saw flashing lights behind my vehicle. I pulled off to the side of the road. The police officer did not get out of his car; in fact, he screamed at me to get out of my car and put my hands up. I looked around, and three more squad cars arrived. I started to shake and did not know what was going on. The officer had me get down on my knees before he approached me. He walked up to me and called me just another gang-banger. I was trying to explain to him that I was dressed like this for school. He replied, "Yeah right, you are." He began to search my car, when I remembered what my teacher, a former police officer, told me to do. I said, "Hey, I am a student. You have no probable cause to search my car." Fortunately, the officer looked up, apologized, and told me to be on my way. Thanks, Teach!

The officer in this scenario catered to a stereotype that assumed the individual had gang relations related to appearance. An effective officer would be cautious in this situation. However, an effective officer would not address an individual with an offensive label. For instance, the movie *The Hurricane*, the story of Ruben Hurricane Carter, brings awareness to the stereotypical nature of society. An innocent man found guilty because of his color sat in prison for 22 years. Stereotyping must desist; not only in the minds of officers, but in the minds of the society. Stereotypes are linked to role expectations, race, and gender issues, ultimately altering perception, which leads to false judgment. Role expectations are driven by the media's labeling of individuals based on speech, gestures, gender, race, and appearance. The more education an officer receives, the less likely one is to adopt this type of behavior. However, some departments only require applicants to hold a high school diploma to work on their force. Becoming educated in the field of social sciences, including criminal justice, is critical to becoming a successful law enforcement official. Until then, the ability to practice critical thinking may be weakened. Therefore, a higher education is critical to those pursuing law enforcement positions.

A filter can thwart the process of communication because a learned response interferes with perception, reliance on facts, and credibility. In contemporary society, it will be difficult not to label, stereotype, expect, or judge; but in this type of field, filters need to be abolished. An altered state of perception leads to an altered state of communication and interpretation, whether receiving or sending. Reece and Meier (1995) examine the impact of communication filters:

When people are influenced by one or more of these filters, their perception of the message may be totally different from what the sender intended to communicate. (p. 33)

Law enforcement recruits must practice techniques that are directed away from filtering agents and toward nonfiltering agents, which will justifiably negate prejudice and engage effective communication. A professional officer may well know after communicating in a natural state whether a threat exists. In addition, a professional officer will allow the subject to determine his or her destiny by allowing him or her a meaningful chance to communicate and comply before catering to the use of force.

Scenario 10: What Is Going On?

An officer pulls over a male driver. The officer senses tension and responds to it by giving orders and yelling at the individual. What the officer does not know is that a wasp has just stung the subject in the foot, and he is having an allergic reaction to the wasp sting. The officer, in a maneuver we have all seen, rips the subject out of the car and handcuffs him until the subject calms down enough to explain. The officer is angry and frustrated, as is the subject.

This behavior is not the officer's fault. This is a learned reaction, which stems from training. A scare tactic is put into the minds of officers: *You never know what you are walking up on.* This is true. However, an officer needs to approach situations with a voice of communication and reason. Therefore, an officer will be alerted to the situation at hand and become aware of how to control it without leaving a negative perception of law enforcement, in turn allowing individuals to be more prone to cooperation and general openness with law enforcement officials. Emotions also filter the process of communication. Because of anger, the subject and the officer were not communicating. A professional officer would have calmed the subject down enough to indeed communicate effectively, and would have sought medical attention for the subject. The same mistake can also occur when using language and nonverbal filters. If a situation occurs where nonverbal gestures are made or a foreign language is spoken, do not hesitate to simply ask, "*Hey, what does that mean?*" or "*Please clarify!*" These statements are very effective. Reece and Brandt determine the impact of nonverbal messages:

Nonverbal messages are messages without words or silent messages. These are the messages (other than spoken or written words) we communicate through facial expressions, voice tone, gestures, appearance, posture, and other nonverbal means. Research indicates that our nonverbal messages have much more impact than verbal messages. (p. 37)

There is an ability to relate to other humans regardless of differences. These filters can be suspended by simply keeping an open mind and asking questions. Again, in regard to nonverbal filters, do not assume that they are threatening because the subject often becomes threatened or on guard around police officers. First and foremost, before acting, communicate.

Scenario 11: I Thought I Understood

> My kids were playing outside while my wife and I were cooking dinner. She was cutting onions, and I was cutting the salad. My wife cut her finger. It was a bad slice, and my youngest son walked into the house. I was angry and told him, "Mommy cut her finger! Call 911." The police arrived, entered my home, and threw me up against the wall. One officer kept yelling at me, "Did you cut your wife? Answer yes or no!" The other officer who was speaking with my children stated, "He is angry!" Every time I attempted to explain what happened, he screamed "Answer yes or no!" I was handcuffed and put in the squad car until they figured out that we were just cooking dinner.

The officers in this scenario assumed that the father was angry and had injured his wife. 911 calls are almost always chaotic, but remaining calm and attempting to rationalize situations are important. A professional officer would ask open-ended questions, which would reveal more information than yes-or-no questions. Say, *"Tell me what happened."* Do not say, *"Did he or she strike you?"* Allow for explanatory answers, and then interpret. Emotions also filter communication. Do not take it for granted that someone is angry or happy; always note a natural state, then seek the pattern of emotion. Offensive discourse could be as meaningless as *"Why are you so mad,"* or *"You look really angry."* These statements in fact can change behavior instantly, most of the time toward the defensive. Maybe now the person becomes angry or even violent. Sometimes what is expected can be easily nudged into becoming reality—the pinnacle of irony. A professional officer caters to discourse that leaves for open-ended answers. Ask open-ended questions.

Assignment Guide Issue 2: Don't Hesitate to Communicate, but Proceed with Caution

Group discussion assignment

- In Scenario 6, is it typical to stereotype individuals based on appearance? What type of training could we implement to change this reaction? Is this possible at all?

- In Scenario 7, how could this have been avoided? What could the officer have done differently?

Humiliation

Issue 3

Scenario 12: Control I Believe

When I was arrested, this officer called me a freak, loser, and a pot-head in front of all my friends.

Scenario 13: Public Humiliation

I was at a party with all my friends when the police arrived. They came to tell us to keep the music down. This one officer recognized me from the time my sister and I were fighting. He said, "Hey John, have yah beat up your sister lately?"

Scenario 14: Powerful Humiliation

I was arrested at a bar for insulting the owner because he continuously watered down drinks. It began as a conversation and turned into a heated argument, and the police were called. I was with my family and friends when the police arrived. The officer did not allow me to give my side of the story. He just humiliated me in front of the entire club. He made statements such as "Who is the tough guy now?" as he grabbed my head and said, "Listen up, loser, I don't care what happened. You're coming with me! Don't you have a record? I thought I arrested you just last week."

A subcultural trait of law enforcement officials is the belief that humiliating a suspect will control situations. Humiliation is thought to weaken the suspect psychologically, which is believed to lessen the officer's chance of a violent interaction. However, the opposite is true. By humiliating a suspect in front of children, family members, and friends, the chances of violence are higher because giving in to insult can challenge one rather than alleviate possible violent behavior. Humiliation is associated with power. Undue power is applied via humiliation, allegedly to weaken a suspect's state of mind. However, this does nothing more than inject violent behavior into the suspect. A professional officer will not resort to verbal or physical forms of humiliation. A professional officer knows that insulting language creates negative outcomes, reinforcing the public's negative perception of law enforcement.

Assignment Guide Issue 3: Humiliation

Group discussion assignment

- In Scenario 14, does this form of public humiliation reflect poorly on law enforcement officers? Why or why not?

- In Scenario 14, how should the officer have handled this situation? How would you have handled this situation?

Public Perception and Fear

Issue 4

Scenario 15: Pull Over Already!

My husband and I were driving to the mall, and our four-year-old child was in the back-seat sleeping when, all of a sudden, we noticed flashing lights behind our vehicle. My husband in his early years was a troublemaker and has a record. He is scared to death when the police pull us over. They treat him differently because he has a record; and he has been harassed and abused before by police officers. However, his glory days were 15 years ago. He decided not to stop, and a chase was initiated. I was screaming at him to stop the vehicle, but he was so scared he would not stop for several minutes. When he finally calmed down and stopped the vehicle, we were bombarded by police officers screaming and yelling at us to get out of the car. My husband did not mean to upset anyone. He was just so scared.

Scenario 16: What Should I Do?

I am working at a bar, and lately this one man keeps coming back to see me. He is odd and gives me the creeps. He stares at me constantly and claims that he knows everything about me. I found out that he is a homicide detective. He makes statements to me such as "I just painted my bedroom blood red. I know everything about you!" He knew my name, where I lived, and even entered my locked car to close my sunroof while I was working. I am terrified because he has access to any and all information about me and my family. He makes it clear to me that he knows everything about me, and every time he comes in, I want to hide. I believe that he is stalking me, and there is nothing that I can do about it because he is above the law. What should I do?

The public has a negative perception of law enforcement, and a fear factor is destroying citizen-officer trust. A professional officer would not abuse the badge to achieve status and/or a date. Furthermore, a professional officer would not physically or mentally abuse a subject. If such actions were reported to the chief of a department, the officer would suffer disciplinary actions.

Breaking the *bad cop* stereotype and beginning to gain citizen trust is indicative of genuine communication and not abusing the badge. If there is a conflict, attempt to persuade through communication. Traditionally, to say less is better, but rage in demanding compliance is an accepted practice. To the contrary, *to say more* is better, with as little rage as possible, because then the situation becomes controlled and does not become an *us* vs. *them*, environment. In fact, when an officer leaves the academy, the first issue addressed by an FTO is the issue of forgetting everything that has been learned via the academy or educationally. Dantzker (1995) reinforces the idea that police subculture has established its own rules and training:

Upon leaving the academy one of the tasks of the field training officer according to Lundman (1980), is to capitalize on the rookies' disenchantment with their training experiences and finalize the rookies' break with the academy experience. There is near consensus among social scientists who have studied police socialization that FTO's tell rookies that the academy experience is a waste of time and to forget all that crap they were told in the academy. (p. 86)

A new police recruit must be willing and ready to fully employ education in response to unwarranted and ineffective FTO tactics and demands.

The sniper incidents around Washington, D.C. gained attention globally. One morning a news radio station was shocked at the public's response. Every single call blamed the police for the sniper incidents. The radio show hosts did nothing more than defend the police during every call that was taken. In fact, the sniper incidents became non-existent in the eyes of America when there was a police officer pictured on the front page of the newspaper pointing a gun at a car. The snipers even left statements blaming the police for not answering telephone calls and having rookie trainees answer the telephones. The talk show hosts had to stop taking callers because every caller made a negative statement geared toward law enforcement officers.

The Son of Sam Killer talks about the Virginia sniper: *"But he said he had been, feeling this person's anger and rage toward law enforcement."* (Zernike, 2002, New York Times)

The public's perception of law enforcement has always been negative, relating to fear and distrust of police officers. The root cause stems from corruption, abuse of power, and law enforcement's authoritarian nature. *To Protect and Serve* is an officer's goal, the law enforcement motto is not intended to scare fellow Americans. Public perception must be bolstered, and by implementing continuous genuine communication techniques and sanctions for abusive behavior, it can be. In the eyes of the public, historically negative stigmas of law enforcement officials still exist.

Assignment Guide Issue 4: Public Perception and Fear

Group discussion assignment

- In your opinion, how does the public view law enforcement officials? What do you believe the overall consensus to be: a beneficial relationship or a negative one?

Teamwork, but I Thought We Were a Team?

Issue 5

Scenario 17: Us vs. Them

I remember when I was at the academy and my instructor continually stated, "Remember, it is us versus them, the bad guys versus the good guys." These statements were drilled into my head over and over again. When I finally reached the street, I couldn't help but look at others as threats. In the back of my mind I felt as though everyone not wearing a uniform was my enemy and not on my team. I felt that my attitude changed toward others, especially when I conversed with others while on duty or while off duty. In addition, I felt that everyone was out to get me, and I could not understand my instructor's philosophy.

Scenario 18: Leads

I tried so hard to become a good federal law enforcement officer. I became an expert on Jonestown Lead, a software program used for identifying suspects. It was a new computerized software program. Therefore, many of the seasoned agents were hesitant in learning how to use it. I took it upon myself to gain viable leads. I was retrieving so many that I decided to begin handing out leads to other agents. However, my generosity sparked argument and hostile attitudes. Shockingly, I realized that a team atmosphere was not in place. In fact, much to my chagrin, I was surrounded by a highly competitive atmosphere that catered to a "me" ideal rather than a "team" ideal.

Scenario 19: Hit and Run

I witnessed an accident and decided to wait for the police to arrive on the scene so that I could elaborate on the facts of the accident. When the officer arrived, I was assisting the woman who was hit by a semi-truck that left the scene. I did manage to get the license plate number of the truck that was involved in this hit-and-run accident. When the officer arrived on the scene, he told me to leave. I tried to explain to him that I witnessed the accident, but he replied, "I will tell you just one more time, if you are not involved in this accident, then leave now!" I took the license plate number home with me. I thought that the officer and I were on the same team.

Scenario 20: Brotherly Love

I love my brother very much, but lately he has been taking drugs. I finally figured out who was giving him the drugs. I called the police and reported the individual. I wanted to remain anonymous, but the officer told me that he would not pursue the incident unless I revealed my identification and assured me that it would be kept private. I gave him my information, but he wanted my date of birth and my address. I felt as though I was being harassed when I was only trying to help. When he found the individual that I reported, he told him that I called the police. I thought I could trust the police. I thought that we were on the same side. My brother has not spoken to me since that incident.

Scenario 21: Powerful Competition

Internally, arrests, tickets, lack of trust, promotions based on production, production based on arrests, and overall factors complementing competition breakdown of the law enforcement team atmosphere exist today. In addition, externally, a powerful persona indicative of curtness, shortness, authoritarianism, and overall a lack of communication is breaking down the team atmosphere associated with the police and the public.

Team: a number of persons associated in some joint action (Webster's Unabridged Dictionary of the English Language, p. 1457).

Part of America's team is law enforcement, for all players cater to one overriding goal: to deter crime and/or interfere with its plans.

So why is the police subculture a team in and of itself? The *Us versus Them, The Art of War,* and *Machiavellian* attitudes still exist. For law enforcement to be effective, a unified team environment needs to be in place. Why don't citizens call in more crimes? Why don't citizens approach officers for help? Because a team atmosphere has not been established, nor is the idea reinforced. Through friendly citizen–officer communication, an effective team atmosphere can be established, resulting in more public trust. O'Brien (1995) examines teamwork: "*Until a group establishes common, shared goals, something all members will be striving to achieve, it is not a team*" (p. 3).

A unified team should have a genesis in place. In pursuance of solving issues through communication and building community support, a need to initiate a team atmosphere is essential. Becoming a team will open up the floodgates of active communication between law enforcement and society. A team actively works together, communicates, and becomes unified through one common goal. Currently, a team atmosphere that encompasses community and law enforcement barely exists. Team building of law enforcement officers and society needs to be influenced, and law enforcement should be initiating this process. By continuously communicating with the public and suspects, law enforcement can slowly build a team ethos. Evidence that a team philosophy can indeed work is nationally noted in the television show *America's Most Wanted*. The show urges Americans to aid in the capture of criminals. This show is a success because it encourages the idea of a unified team: police and the American people. Every law enforcement team would benefit by employing a "John Walsh" behavior, which is essential in establishing a team network and bolstering the public's perception of law enforcement.

Becoming a team player will demand the will to communicate with suspects/offenders. O'Brien (1995) analyzes conflict in a team atmosphere:

The paralyzing effect of conflict seems to be related to the size of the conflict, and conflicts have a way of growing. The longer we try to bury them, the bigger they get. What starts off as a slight difference of opinion becomes the principle of the thing and a minor, somewhat annoying personality trait leads to an intense dislike of the person exhibiting the trait. (p. 71)

This distasteful trait, when applied to law enforcement officers, can provoke their powerful nature rather than a communicative, comforting, team-player attitude and understanding nature; which, in turn, would calm a situation and not exacerbate it. If a communicative approach were taken, then the goals of breaking the *bad cop* stereotype, bolstering citizen trust, establishing a team atmosphere, and thereby crime would decrease. With continuous, positive communication by law enforcement officials directed toward the exercise of a unified team atmosphere, all of the above-mentioned goals would be achieved.

Assignment Guide Issue 5: Teamwork, but I Thought We Were a Team?

Group discussion assignment

- In your opinion, does a police subculture still exists? Why or why not?
- Do you think police officers lose friends upon entering the field of law enforcement? Why or why not?
- Why is the ideal of team so important in law enforcement? List the reasons for your answer.
- Why is the ideal of team important with the community? List the reasons for your answer.

Part II

Problem Solve, and Persuade with a Genuine Attitude

"Let us never negotiate out of fear. But let us never fear to negotiate."

— John F. Kennedy

"We have thought of peace as passive and war as the active way of living. The opposite is true. War is not the most strenuous life. It is a kind of rest cure compared to the task of reconciling our differences. From war to peace is ... from futile to the effective, from the strategic to the active, from the destructive to the creative way of life. ... The world will be regenerated by the people who rise above these passive ways and heroically seek, by whatever hardship, by whatever toil, the methods by which people can agree."

— Mary Parker Follett

Style and Effectiveness: Your Attitude

Issue 6

"Peacemaking is the art and science of weaving and reweaving oneself with others into a social fabric of mutual love, respect, and concern."

— Bruce A. Arrigo

Scenario 22: Traffic Stop or Bust

> A woman was driving on a busy road, with her seven-year-old son in the back seat. She was pulled over by a police officer. The officer approached her car and yelled, "Is this your boy? It's obvious that you don't care about him. Give me your driver's license now! You are obviously trying to kill your own kid!"

In this scenario, the driver had her son seat belted in the backseat. The child began to cry as the officer yelled at his mother. The officer was attacking her parenting. Regardless the act of the offender, it is not an officer's duty to pass judgment on a suspect/offender. The woman allegedly ran a red light. Assume the driver did run a red light. Would there be grounds for an officer to approach the car and attack her parenting practices? Of course it is agreed that a risk factor was apparent, but an officer's job is to alert one to their mistake and ticket accordingly or issue a warning. However, this officer decided to overstep his bounds by verbally attacking the driver's parenting, which alarmed the driver even more than the thought of a ticket. The officer's comments were needless and offensive, which then led to a heated argument and an upset child.

Upon approach, a negative attitude toward a suspect/offender will do nothing more than cause confusion and argument. This approach in and of itself is offensive. A professional law enforcement official will not approach another individual with personal verbal attacks, an elevated voice level, or insinuations of bad parenting, especially in front of a child. In addition, this incident possibly thwarted any chance of continued reinforcement in the child's mind that police officers are genuinely trustworthy individuals.

The driver contacted the police chief and filed a formal grievance against this officer. This officer has had several complaints of the same nature and a history of calling people *bad* parents. The chief recommended that the officer apologize to the child and possibly be put on suspension. Whether an individual ran a red light or not, the officer's insulting approach was out of line, negative in effect, and demeaning in nature. Therefore, a negative outcome establishing a heated argument, a frightened child, and a negative perception of law enforcement was reinforced.

A professional officer would have approached the vehicle, identified himself to the mother and child, reminding the driver that by not acknowledging traffic signals, accidents do occur. For example: *"Hi, how are we doing today? Hi sport, my name is Officer X. Miss Jones, did you know that accidents occur from not obeying traffic signals? Try to be more careful. To make sure you're a bit more careful, I'm going to issue you a ticket. Okay, have a good day."*

Let's assume that the driver stated, *"But I did not run a red light!"*

The reply, *"My job is to be observant, and unfortunately, I believe differently, okay? I must do my job and issue you a ticket."*

Explanatory discourse along with a courteous approach will leave an individual speechless and bolster citizen good perception of policing officials. The approach is important and will shape genuine outcomes.

Scenario 23: Mean Old Cop

A student was pulled over for speeding. The officer approached his vehicle, and the student said, "How are you?" The officer stated, "Better than you're going to be doing. Shut up and give me your license!"

In scenario 23, the student was asked if he would still think of the officer as a jerk if the officer would have replied that he was doing well (instead of his snide reply), explained that the student could have caused an accident, and that fatalities occur from speeding. The driver replied, "No," and explained that a friendly approach rather than an offensive one would have been more productive. When given the opportunity to see it in a different light, the driver felt differently about the scenario.

Again, the officer approached the vehicle replying with an offensive comment rather than explaining his duty in a respectful and courteous manner, and just doing his job professionally.

A fear factor has been instilled in the average citizen, thus on approach a respectful discourse is needed. Offering an explanation will in turn calm a situation. Attitudes shape outcomes and processes of communication. Attitude is the most important part of the job. A bad attitude provokes negative outcomes.

Charles Swindoll is credited with saying:

The longer I live, the more I realize the impact of attitude on life. Attitude is more important than appearance, giftedness, or skill. For example, people who go through life with a positive mental attitude see daily obstacles as opportunities rather than road blocks and therefore, are more likely to achieve their personal and professional goals. People who filter their daily experiences through a negative attitude tend to focus on what is going wrong and find it difficult to achieve contentment or satisfaction in any aspect of their lives. It makes no difference how attractive, intelligent, or skilled they are; their attitude holds them back. (Reece & Brandt, 2002, p. 145)

A professional officer is aware that a positive attitude provokes a positive response. Reece and Brandt define attitude.

An attitude is a relatively strong belief or feeling toward a person, object, idea, or event. It is an emotional readiness to behave in a particular manner. Values serve as a foundation for attitudes, and attitudes serve as a foundation for behavior. (p. 145)

Scenario 24: You're Under Arrest

I happened to be watching a cop show on TV the other night, and saw an officer pull over a speeding car. The suspect was standing outside of the car and cooperating. After the officer checked the suspect's driver's license number he noticed that a warrant for the suspect was outstanding. He walked over to the suspect and stated, "You're going with me now! You're under arrest." The suspect fled, jumped over a barricade, and was injured with two broken legs.

In scenario 24 the approach should have been, *"Sir, there is a discrepancy with your license. Let's remain calm and figure out what the issue is. We can work it out. Please come with me so that we can straighten this matter out."*

An officer must first try to alleviate fear factors and then follow procedure. How many possible issues could be lingering in a suspect's mind? Is this officer corrupt? Is this officer going to abuse me? The media has cast a negative perception of law enforcement. Veteran officers trained in the reform/professional era of policing are retiring, along with their traditional attitudes. A new generation of officers stand hated, having to correct traditional negative stigmas. By befriending suspects, a wealth of information can be collected; perhaps beneficially capturing criminals and deterring crime. This friendly approach in and of itself will be effective if it's not authoritarian or abusive in nature. Professional officers will adopt a respectful discourse and maintain a positive attitude as the social era (1980) of policing has surfaced and community policing is now at the forefront of our agenda, which aids in creating an amicable officer.

Negative police attitudes originated from a military structure, one ready for war. If ready for war, one is ready to *kill or be killed*. Throughout life, values are shaped by family, mentors, and peer groups. This in turn shapes attitudes, which shape behaviors. Early American policing was highly corrupt; in fact, one had to pay money to even become a police officer because it was a political position of power. Walker (1992) examines early policing:

Officers were selected entirely on the basis of their political connections. In New York City, a $300.00 payment to the Tammany Hall political machine was the only requirement for appointment to the force. (p. 11)

There was no training and/or educational requirement. There was no supervision for these officers. Their job was based on politics; therefore, discrimination, abuse, and corruption ran rampant. Citizens regarded police officers as political figures, deficient in the "protect and serve" duty category.

At the beginning of the twentieth century, law enforcement went through a change. This change demanded that the quality of policing be enhanced. This is where we will note a serious mistake. August Vollmer, superintendent of the District of Columbia police force, 1898–1915, provoked this professional movement. Vollmer was responsible for most positive change in policing. In fact, he began the first school that taught criminal justice. He advocated higher education for police officers. Vollmer's reform agenda had seven points to be addressed: eliminating political influence, appointing qualified officers, catering to nonpartisan public servants, heightening personnel standards, introducing different management styles, developing different units, and–the cancer that has now poisoned law enforcement officers today—military-style discipline. This agenda demonstrated change and is relevant even today. Rather than appealing to the idea of a police officer acting as a public servant, we redirected their mission toward that of a paramilitary-type individual. We need to remedy this practice and we have done so when we entered the social era of policing (1980), which now has introduced the community policing. Because of negative history, law enforcement has suffered, we now witness attitudes scorched by hate toward police officers. Moreover, this militant ideal rather than that of a public servant and team player has provoked negative learned responses from the public in turn, shaping law enforcement's negative attitude toward civilians.

Police reform progressed very slowly. By 1920 only a few departments [in] Milwaukee, Cincinnati, and Berkley could be labeled professional. In most other cities police departments remained mired in corruption. Chicago seemed to resist all efforts at reform. Despite all failures, the reformers could claim one great success: They firmly established professionalism as an ideal, and their agenda dominated police reform for decades. (Walker)

Again in the 1960s, we noticed a reform movement. The Supreme Court became involved in police procedures and constitutional standards, including due process of law. Regardless, police corruption persisted. Riots between the police and African-Americans occurred almost daily. Shootings of African-Americans happened often. A new age of reform began, and along with it many organizations were formed in the areas of research, law enforcement educational programs, police foundations, and crime commissions; overall personnel practices were restructured. Today, we still face old problems, just new agendas. We battle gang violence and terrorism. We need a new agenda. Walker said:

In the first problem orientated police experiment, officers in Newport News, Virginia, attacked crime in a deteriorated housing project by helping the residents organize to improve the project itself."

Restructuring our policing agenda is under way. By restructuring our agenda and by targeting a public service platform of effectiveness, public trust will be enhanced. This ideal not only reforms police attitude but will reform attitudes of society. The negative aspects of policing history make it difficult to change the attitudes and disposition of the public. However, police attitudes toward the job need to dismiss curtness, disdain, and authoritarian/militant behavior. Attitudes should reflect a willingness to help others as public servants by becoming a mentor, mediator, problem solver, and/or manager as reflected in today's agenda of community policing.

Police attitudes need to become positive, not negative. Have you ever heard a police officer say, *"How can I feel positive after the day is over as I deal with negativity every day?"* The job does not have to be negative. Why not ask yourself at the end of your shift how many people you helped today? How many problems did you solve? Did your positive attitude rub off on any one else? Did your positive attitude affect others? Maintain a positive attitude when dealing with others. Try smiling when you are asked a question or are responding to one. A need to change focus by establishing more serviceable attitudes is at hand. A need to dismiss practices of angry militant conduct is present.

Assignment Guide Issue 6: Style and Effectiveness: Your Attitude

Group discussion assignment

- In class, please role play Scenario 22 and determine how you would have approached the vehicle.

- In class, please role play Scenario 24 and determine how you would have handled the situation.

A Negotiating Behavior

"This mistake is dedicated to all law enforcement officers who deal with conflict daily and to those individuals who are committed to resolving issues, mediating disturbances, and working cooperatively with the public. An officer must find solutions to problems without creating more conflict. By appealing to authoritarian methods, officers create unnecessary conflict. Officers need to improve their negotiating strategies to include analysis of behavior. Methods by which law enforcement approaches societal issues, communicates, and resolves issues should be that of a negotiator."

— K. Karlberg

Scenario 25: Do Not Fear to Negotiate

You approach a drug sale in progress. The money is in sight, and the drugs are changing hands. Both individuals are arrested. The Miranda Rights have been read. You are at the station, and interrogation begins. You have a hunch about the big boss but you need a name. Instead of threatening, yelling, and invoking fear in the suspect, why not sit down and begin talking about drug overdoses of teenagers, drug-related shootings, and citing other examples of drug problems? Next, ask for help. Ask: Why? How? Be friendly; be a good listener; personalize a story about yourself. Understand; ask questions; make sure that the individual is told that he or she is doing the right thing. Act in a way of aiding, not threatening. The answers one needs will be given with names and valid addresses.

Scenario 26: I Like My Music Loud!

I like my music loud, but my neighbors don't and they always call the police. The police routinely come to my door, telling me to turn off my music. One day a police officer came over asking me about my music and when I play it, then telling me that she would be back in a minute. When she came back she told me that the neighbors will allow me to play my music anytime Friday or Saturday, but not on Monday and Wednesday from 5 p.m. to 9:30 p.m. I agreed—problem solved. Thanks, officer!

Scenario 27: Halloween

Known offenders tend to repeat their offenses on Halloween. Parents allow their children to stay out late at night. Kids egg houses and harass other kids. Even when they get caught, they never get in trouble because police officials just call their parents to pick them up. However, this year was different. As an officer, I decided to visit a known offender's home before Halloween and suggested we negotiate a trade-off. If this repeat juvenile offender gets caught again this year egging houses and, I clearly stated, beating up children, he will have to clean up the neighborhood dog feces during the winter months as a community service project. Know your community.

Dogs barking, kids fighting, friends quarreling, neighbors disputing. General negotiations exist in the day and life of an officer. Negotiation is highlighted in law schools, but severely neglected in police academies. This is a learned process relating *service* in a different fashion. The power of negotiation is critical in police work. Fisher, Ury, and Patton (1991) examine negotiation: *"How one negotiates and how one prepares to negotiate can make an enormous difference, whatever the relative strengths of each party"* (p. 3).

The ability to persuade someone to do or not to do something is the art of negotiation.

If you understand the other side and they understand you; if emotions are acknowledged and people are treated with **respect** *even when they disagree; if there is clear two-way communication with good listening; and if people problems are dealt with directly, not by demanding or offering concessions on substance, negotiations are likely to be smoother and more successful for both parties.* (p. 6)

Recall the citizen fear factor previously identified by using the technique of negotiation. Fisher, Ury, and Patton (1991) claim that negotiation can eliminate the fear factor and enhance citizen trust:

A message does not have to be unequivocal to be clear and effective. In many cases, helping the other side understand your thinking—even when you are of two minds about something—can reduce fears, clear up misconceptions, and promote joint problem solving. (p. 4)

If an officer approaches a situation and begins to ask questions and then listens attentively, the situation does not become challenging for the suspect and lessens the thought of rebellion, because a negotiating philosophy promotes a less threatening atmosphere. This philosophy is emphasized by Fisher, Ury, and Patton (1991):

Showing that you have heard the other side also increases your ability to persuade them. When the other side feels heard by you, they are more apt to listen to you. Once the other side knows that you understand what they have said, they cannot dismiss your disagreement as simple lack of understanding. (p. 7)

Service can be applied in understanding how to negotiate effectively rather than applying physical power. Influencing the individual through negotiation techniques is a key factor in becoming a successful police officer. The worst-case scenario is when a suspect becomes noncompliant and will not cooperate in the negotiation process; subsequently, the use of force must surface. Simple techniques such as sympathizing with the suspect and negotiating peaceful resolutions will help in obtaining more information than strong-arm tactics or threatening suspects who do not comply. In addition, a negotiating behavior will create a positive perception of law enforcement officials.

At this juncture one cannot focus on outcomes; however, the process of negotiation should be examined. Outcomes mean the process is finished. On the other hand, processes are ongoing, with the potential of being finished. Cooperative negotiating tactics can resolve issues and bolster citizen trust. A study conducted by Gerald R. Williams (1993) concluded that noncombative negotiators will be successful:

We received a total of 351 completed questionnaires, giving us that number of very richly detailed descriptions of negotiations who were considered effective by their peers. In our review of the literature, we had hypothesized that the results would show that cooperative approaches to negotiation were more effective than tough or combative approaches. (p. 157)

The cooperative-style negotiator is an effective negotiator, and Williams has described traits that pertain to this type of negotiator: trustworthy, ethical, fair, courteous, personable, sociable, friendly, gentle, obliging, patient, forgiving, intelligent, dignified, and self-controlled (p. 160). Working toward genuine outcomes will not be difficult if a cooperative personality is at the forefront of an officer's agenda. Williams (1993) claims a win-win negotiating technique is possible:

Cooperatives *are quintessential win-win negotiators. On the other hand, effective aggressive negotiators see it completely differently. Their attitude is this, if all you want me to do is go around making everybody feel good about themselves, you don't need me. … It's not worth getting up in the morning for; it's not a serious objective. So they are win-lose negotiators; they want a clear winner and a clear loser; if the score is still tied, then the game's not over yet; you have to go into overtime."* (p. 161)

In the criminal justice field, the cooperative approach works best; however, employing an aggressive approach in some instances might be necessary, but save it as a last resort. Allow the subject to choose his or her destiny by giving him or her an initial chance at a peaceful resolution. Williams claims that 99 percent of the time, a cooperative approach is effective and an aggressive approach is ineffective: *"One reason that ineffective aggressive negotiators are so obnoxious or irritating is that they make unreasonable opening demands or offers"* (p. 163).

Demanding on approach leaves an individual angry and in turn can cause serious negative consequences. Proceed with caution when using an aggressive approach because weapons are easily accessible to the public, and retaliation might surface. Williams (1993) establishes objectives of a cooperative negotiator, and they are as follows: *"If I am fair and trustworthy; if I make unilateral concessions; then the other side will feel an irresistible moral obligation to reciprocate"* (p. 167). Professional officers will adopt approachable, cooperative negotiating styles.

Assignment Guide Issue 7: A Negotiating Behavior

Group discussion assignment

- At times law enforcement officers encounter issues that require the use of discretion. What is discretion? Please read Scenario 27. How would you handle juveniles' vandalizing behavior during Halloween?

- What ideas do you have to deter juvenile delinquency during Halloween? Please generate ideas and discuss.

Mediate/Conflict Resolution

Issue 8

"We see ever increasing urgency in mediating, cutting across, and reducing these imbalances for the very sake of human survival."

— Bruce A. Arrigo

"Mediation requires listening emphatically and respectfully to the power holders' response and ultimately listening most carefully and respectfully to one's harshest or most immediate critics. As one learns what the opposing parties' interests are, one's own direct and vicarious experience of choice(s), when discussed in relationship to the choices of others, can assist the conflicting parties in developing a repertoire of options."

— Bruce A. Arrigo

Scenario 28: Cheerleading

It was the night of cheerleading practice. A call came into the station from the local school that parents were fighting at the school. I arrived at the scene to find five sets of parents standing inside the school, outside of the gym, and they were heckling the coach and participants. Some of the parents' children were former participants but were dismissed from the cheerleading team for various violations. The team was very spirited and competed nationally. Therefore, the stakes were high. I sensed jealousy, outrage, and hostile attitudes. I told everyone to leave immediately or they would be arrested.

If the officer instead would have stood patiently listening for a short time to the parents venting their frustration about the team and certain student participants and then explained to the parents that by acting in such a way in front of 50 youngsters that their behavior was negatively affecting the kids, and that a more appropriate time and place for conflict resolution should be established. Thus, a positive perception of the officer and a less hostile environment could have been established. Perhaps, if the officer would have elected a credible parent to coordinate a time and place for a mediation process in which the officer was free to assist, a peaceful resolution might have been established.

Scenario 29: Rake Your Own Leaves

A call came in that neighbors were disputing. One neighbor claimed that the other neighbor continuously threw leaves into his yard instead of bagging them himself. Both parties were elderly and very angry. The receiver of the leaves insisted that the leaf-thrower should be arrested for trespassing and littering. After speaking to the leaf-thrower, I realized that, due to his age, it was too difficult for him to bag all the leaves in his yard; therefore, simply tossing them into his next-door neighbor's yard was a healthier option. I told the leaf-thrower to stop throwing leaves into the neighbor's yard or he would be arrested.

If the officer instead had explained to the receiving party that the elderly man had health issues and simply could not bag his own leaves, requesting that the receiver allow the thrower to set a can by the fence on leaf raking day so the elderly raker could put his leaves in the can, that could have solved the dispute. In addition, if the officer requested a favor of the receiver, such as tying the knot on the bag and setting it over the fence for the elderly man so that he could dispose of it, the issue could have been resolved.

Scenario 30: Paint Ball

It's summer, and all the kids are out of school. A call came in that a child was firing a gun that was spraying some sort of paint all over the caller's home. On arriving at the scene, I observed pink paint everywhere, including splattered on the house of the caller. A young boy just received a gift from his aunt, a paintball gun. I confiscated the paint ball gun.

A productive outcome could have been established if, instead, the officer had asked the child's parents to have the child clean the paint off the elderly caller's home and apologize to her. To enhance officer perception, one could have suggested that the child set up a target surrounded by wooden boards and plastic, rather than target practicing on houses.

Furthermore, if the officer explained the danger of paintballs, reemphasized protective gear, and spoke to the parents about supervision about only target shooting in a designated, secured, and protected area, that would have reinforced a peaceful resolution. Continuing, the officer could have suggested to the parents a contract between the parents and child stipulating the requirements, which would have allowed, if obeyed, the continued use of the paintball gun.

Scenario 31: Spanish Lesson

Today I was a mediator. I was on duty when a man came running down the escalator yelling at me. He proceeded to tell me that he was upstairs in the restaurant and that a couple of Hispanic employees were bad-mouthing him in Spanish. What the employees did not know was that the individual was Cuban, and spoke fluent Spanish. I do not wish to repeat what was allegedly said. It was so shocking that I was at a loss of words, and the only thing I could say to this tourist was that I was sorry. I calmed the tourist and walked him upstairs, wrote down the names of the employees in question, took down the supervisor's phone number and location, and gave the information to the tourist. When it was all said and done he looked at me and said in broken English, "Thank you,

I liked the way you handled this." I told the workers in Spanish that many people speak Spanish and to be very careful what they say when others are present! They apologized to the tourist.

At times a law enforcement officer becomes a mediator of a conflict between individuals. When a call comes in for a dispute between neighbors or between spouses, it's those kinds of calls that suggest a high probability of violence. However, there are methods that will help resolve the tension between parties. Law enforcement officers make choices and have discretion in implementing solvable alternatives. Police officers need to be able to mediate conflict and apply decision-making techniques. They need to be able to suggest alternatives and implement solutions. Harris (1990) suggests that a peaceful person who uses and encourages peaceful rhetoric motivates peaceful resolutions: *"Such a disposition would orient a person towards caring for others, using compassion, respecting diversity, seeking non-violent alternatives, and mediating conflicts"* (p. 255).

Police officers need to foster peaceful conflict resolution. Conflict resolution involves mediating disputes, which requires a level-headed officer; one who maintains control and who can reasonably analyze situations. A professional officer will deescalate rather than escalate a situation. Peaceful rhetoric is effective in these tense situations. Furthermore, conflict can lead to violent outcomes.

Arrigo (1999) reemphasizes the growing concern pertaining to conflict resolution in the criminal justice field:

We are only too aware of the escalating nature of violence in domestic situations, in street corner encounters, with police-citizen transactions, with guard-prisoner exchanges, with prisoner-prisoner encounters, and generally with various interactions citizens have with criminal justice system and its operatives. (p. 211)

Police officers deal with violent situations on a daily basis. Police officers need to use language that promotes peace, which will deescalate situations and provide for nonviolent outcomes. Arrigo (1999) examines the de-escalation of violence in the butterfly catastrophe model applied to peace making:

It is time to explore the possibilities of applying the butterfly catastrophe model to methods of decreasing interpersonal violence. This will be an important addition for those who have focused on conflict regulation, mediation, and resolution. (p. 204–205)

The butterfly catastrophe is assisted by the cusp catastrophe; concentration on the butterfly catastrophe highlighting the pocket of compromise will be examined. Application of the butterfly catastrophe provides suggestions for peaceful rhetoric that can de-escalate conflict and produce nonviolent outcomes. The butterfly factor is indicative of peaceful discourse. For instance, Arrigo (1999) explains that if discourse relating to restricting a subject's outlet (For example: *"You are under arrest"*) is at hand, it limits the subject's options and consequently a violent attack would have a high probability of occurring (p. 213). On the other hand, when an individual feels that he or she has alternatives of escaping, then violence is less likely to occur (see scenario #24). Katz (1988) has shown that uncontrolled emotions can lead to rage and violent attacks. The works of Katz (1988), Matza (1969), and others *"indicate that a certain moment in the escalation process, the person finds him- or herself more object than subject. Creating time intervals or time lags may provide the pause or space necessary for returning the pacified subject to a reclaimed active position of agent"* (Arrigo, 1999, p. 220).

Arrigo (1996) emphasizes that discourse can produce behavioral effects:

In other words, when a person speaks, she or he takes up temporary residence in a language system that ensures the relative stability of that grammar and that discourse's limited meanings. Discourse, in this view, is performative: it produces effects in behavior.

Arrigo (1999) suggests a peace rhetoric. Harris (1990) also suggests peaceful rhetoric: *"As he indicates, such a disposition would orient a person towards caring for others, using compassion, respecting diversity, seeking non-violent alternatives, and mediating conflicts"* (p. 255).

Furthermore, Harris (1988) says, *"[P]eace, a concept which motivates the imagination … implies human beings working together to resolve conflicts, respect standards of justice, satisfy basic needs, and honor human rights"* (p. 7). In simplifying the butterfly catastrophe, the divergence of peaceful discourse must surface when fostering mediation, conflict resolution, negotiation, and overall discourse. As stated previously, when a subject feels that limitations are being enforced, a negative outcome is highly probable. When less perceived limitations exist, a less likely chance of a negative outcome is probable. Where limitations accompanied by mirrored discourse occur, violence is more likely. However, when fewer restrictions are placed on the subject, along with subsequent peaceful rhetoric, a positive outcome is more likely to occur. Arrigo (1999) highlights the fact that the pocket of compromise has not reached a place of stability, and the pocket may quickly close. However, if given the chance, an officer should rip open the pocket of compromise by perpetuating peaceful rhetoric. Arrigo claims that even though chances of irritation might occur, there is less likelihood of violence occurring. However, the peace rhetoric is still having some effect in producing agitation (highly probable) rather than violence (less probable) (p. 219). Peaceful discourse as reinforced in previous chapters can de-escalate conflicting situations. A professional officer will cater to peaceful rhetoric rather than authoritarian/threatening discourse when mediating and resolving conflict.

Once an officer resolves the conflict and implements a solution, he or she must be able to act on the decision:

To look is one thing. To see what you are looking at is another. To really understand what you see is a third. To learn from what you understand is something else again. But to act on what you have learned is all that truly matters." (LeBoeuf, 1985)

Therefore, officers must have choices and alternatives and possess the behavior and discretion to act on said decisions. More (1984) examines the act of decision making:

While all of us make variety of personal decisions, only about 10 percent of the members of any organized work group have the ability and the desire to exercise formal decision making authority. (p. 289)

There is an obvious lack of specification in this area, which in turn produces ambiguity and vagueness and becomes an enigma for law enforcement officers. Decision-making policies in regard to mediating conflict resolution should be implemented and customized by a degree model. We need creative individuals who can mediate and resolve conflict, persuade, and negotiate. In addition, the implementation of critical reasoning, mediation, and negotiation techniques needs to be introduced into academies. The job of police officer should not belong to the high school graduate because one does not properly learn how to critically evaluate until a higher learning experience is acquired. Police leadership officials need to trust scholarly officers with decision-making, mediation, and conflict-resolution techniques. Furthermore, administration should not advocate limited speech, use of force, authoritarianism, and curtness. Internal police administration needs to allow officers the discretion in making choices. Internal factors need to:

1. Specify goals and missions.

2. Allow for discretion to aid officers in feeling comfortable carrying out their duties.

3. Initiate a higher level of autonomy.

4. Grant leeway regarding departmental policies and regulations.

5. Make resources available to aid officers in obtaining information on decision making regarding precedent.

6. Require more education, which will limit needless and traditional training efforts.

7. Find academies that foster reasoning, communication, decision making, conflict resolution, and negotiation techniques.

8. Revamp award systems to honor those for decision-making, negotiation, mediation, and conflict-resolution techniques. Instead of how many arrests the officer made this month, reward the officer for how many incidents he or she resolved.

9. Request detailed reports on how the officer deterred the crime or negotiated a peaceful resolution.

10. Create a non-authoritarian officer, team player and a community orientated officer.

All these factors will aid in changing the steel tone of law enforcement to a more peaceful one, which in turn will bring a new world of information to the officer, enhance citizen perception, and create a safer environment. Mediation/conflict resolution requires identifying problems, creating solutions to those problems, and implementing the solution to resolve the problem. Thus, mediation/conflict resolution consists of:

1. Identifying the problem.

2. Creating the solution.

3. Accessing the solution.

4. Reevaluating the solution.

5. Acting on the solution.

6. Accomplishing the solution.

7. Accepting negative feedback.

8. Adjusting the solution (if needed).

Assignment Guide Issue 8: Mediate/Conflict Resolution

Group discussion assignment

- Please read Scenario 30. How would you have handled Scenario 30?

- Your instructor will give you scenarios involving two individuals arguing. How would you mediate these disputes quickly and effectively?

Part III

Humanize Oneself

"An officer is not above the law and must approach tasks in a state of awareness rather than a state of disregard."

— K. Karlberg

"Man is the only animal that can remain on friendly terms with the victims he intends to eat until he eats them."

— Samuel Butler

"Man is a rational animal who always loses his temper when he is called upon to act in accordance with the dictates of reason."

— Oscar Wilde

Need Identification

Issue 9

Scenario 32: I Was Robbed

We were being robbed. I woke up to see my husband face down from a blow to the head. I dialed 911, the robber fled, but my husband was severely injured. I was hysterical. When the officer arrived on the scene, he told me to get back, stay away, and knock it off. The ambulance arrived. I left with the ambulance for the hospital. I received not one comforting word from that officer.

Scenario 33: I Need My Insulin

I was leaving a department store when their loss prevention agent approached me and asked me to return to the store with him. I did so. He accused me of shoplifting and was reviewing a tape when I alerted him that I was diabetic and needed my insulin injection. He ignored me. I repeatedly requested that my handcuffs be removed so that I could administer the injection. I sat for an hour begging for my injection. Eventually I lapsed into seizure and woke up in the hospital. Thank you for the $1 million settlement!

Humanize means "to make human and/or personal." The question is: How can we productively interact with others while maintaining a natural state?

A natural state is neither aggressive nor passive. It's a natural state of awareness directed toward the other individual's persona. There are four components to humanizing oneself: improving interpersonal communication (which was addressed in Part I); identifying needs of others; being ethical in nature, which we discuss in Part IV; and learning that my attitude will shape outcomes (Part II).

If a police officer is in the midst of an encounter, he or she must address the needs of a subject. Every person has needs, and if one can identify another's needs, positive outcomes may be brought about quickly. Furthermore, by identifying a need, a calmer and more cooperative suspect will be noted.

The sniper incidents in Washington, D.C. were devastating to society. Psychologists were interviewed, and they were asked to explain why someone would want to randomly kill their fellow citizens. Psychologists stated that this sniper probably was withdrawn, had a family crisis in his or her life, had a dark side, or someone did not notice that something in this person's life had gone severely wrong.

Identifying the needs of others creates a motivational force indicative of cooperation. Abraham Maslow (1943) argued that all individuals have needs, including physical and psychological needs, that affect their behavior. He identified five basic needs. Police officers need to be concerned with two types of needs: higher-order needs and physical needs. Higher-order needs consist of prestige, recognition, self-image, self-confidence, self-worth, belonging, esteem, self-actualization, and any individual behavioral need. For our purposes, physical needs are defined as medical attention and/or illness. Tosi, Rizzo, and Carroll (1986) conclude *"that there is empirical support for need theory and, in particular, Maslow's conceptualization of need theory"* (p. 221).

A police officer as a human being has a duty to interact with other human beings and, in stressful situations, has a duty to appeal to comfort. A professional officer will begin by identifying the needs of subjects/offenders during the initial interaction, and by doing so, a motivated cooperative environment can be created. A professional officer will provide suggestions, whether they relate to medical attention, shelter, food, drug treatment programs, employment, rehabilitation facilitation, health and human services, and/or departments of child welfare. A professional officer will not hesitate to assist a fellow citizen, regardless of the need. A professional officer will take the time to identify the needs of a victim, suspect, and offender. In turn, this leaves the subject with a genuinely positive impression of law enforcement, which bolsters public perception. Identifying the needs and catering to the need in turn bolsters the subject's motivation, denoting that someone cares about the subject (that in itself could be the need), which leaves the subject motivated to do the right thing. A professional officer will not disregard an emotional victim, an injured suspect, and an offender who needs medication or guidance.

Assignment Guide Issue 9: Need Identification

Group discussion assignment

- Does safety come first in any situation? Why or why not?

- Is a part of your duty to ensure public safety?

- Your chief phones you and asks you to take paperwork to the courthouse ASAP. It is important paperwork and you only have a 10-minute window. In route you see a 10-year-old boy who rode his bike into a tree. Do you stop to offer your service or keep going?

Humanize Oneself Through Community Affairs

Issue 10

Scenario 34: Friend or Enemy?

I was assigned to work the Labor Day community picnic. As a new recruit, I stood and observed seasoned officers. I noticed that they stood guarded from the community. They looked mean and remote and did not speak to the members of the community. When someone would ask them a question they would reply, "Do I look like the information desk?"

Scenario 35: The Carnival

It was summertime, and all the carnivals were planned. I was assigned to work at the local carnival for the weekend. Many officers stood in a circle and talked all night. I decided to meet the community, walked around, found trouble, and expressed concern. I found out that on Saturday a fight was planned. I found out that the carnival workers were exposing themselves to children in the outhouses, and discovered that the more individuals I spoke too, the more information I gained.

In this scenario, officers who stood in a corner all night and chose not to humanize themselves failed in the social aspect of their job. Officers who decided to cross the line, so to speak, gained valuable information by interacting with community members. An officer should always want to be aware of his or her surroundings and speak to as many individuals as possible. Hyper-awareness is a survival necessity for any law enforcement official. When speaking, kindness accompanied by respectfulness is important. A professional officer will not alienate him- or herself from the community, but will interact with the public whenever an opportunity arises. Thus, the public reacts positively and feels comfortable in sharing information. Engagement in everyday dialog with members of the community can lead to life-saving information, just by maintaining a hyper-aware persona.

Assignment Guide Issue 10: Humanize Oneself Through Community Affairs

Group discussion assignment

- Should officers be friendly while on duty and in the public eye?
- Should officers wave and shake hands with community members while on duty?
- Should officers speak with citizens informally while on duty? Why or why not?

Community Policing

Issue 11

Scenario 36: Community Policing or Window Dressing

> I remember as a new recruit delivering flyers every summer to every house in the city. It was an extra assignment paid for by grant money. The flyers were a survey about the actions of the police in the community. The survey was entitled Community Policing. When we retrieved the flyers, negative flyers about officers were tossed into the garbage. In fact, one citizen asked me to document a personal complaint about an officer. When I finished, my sergeant directed me to destroy the complaint.

Community policing is no longer a vague term, and is actively practiced in many different forms in almost every department. Ideally, community policing should enhance a citizen–police relationship. In the 1980s, we entered an era of *community policing*. The community era brought the ideal of a partnership with our community to the forefront of our agenda. Community policing is a philosophy that promotes the principle of a community partnership to address crime. Traditionally law enforcement was reactive in its approach to crime; today the ideal of community-oriented policing focuses on a problem-solving approach and uses a proactive approach to fighting crime. Some ideas have led to block captains, community watch programs, citizen academies, and an overall agenda of service for the citizens of the community. Community policing should be linked to a relationship with its citizens on an intimate level. A professional law enforcement agency is aware that an intimate relationship with the public should be established through community policing. Furthermore, a professional police department realizes that a community policing window dressing in exchange for grant funds does not enhance citizen–police relationships and fails in pursuit of bolstering citizen perception of police officers.

In 1987 Eck and Spelman developed the SARA model, which is used as a step-by-step guide to problem-solving policing. The SARA model highlights four strategies: (1) Scanning—examining groups of incidents and identifying the problems; (2) Analyzing—keeping your data and collecting data from all sources; 3) Responding—implementing the solutions, and; (4) evaluating your solutions.

Simple, creative solutions sought by law enforcement officers can enhance citizen perception and create an amicable environment. A professional officer will verbally establish relationships with citizens by creating solutions for their disputes. A professional officer will become an advisor, mediator, negotiator, and problem-solver, and will conform to the community policing philosophy by seeking partnerships with community members.

Assignment Guide Issue 11: Community Policing

Group discussion assignment

- What is community policing?
- What is community-oriented policing?
- In your opinion, does community-oriented policing work?
- What is the SARA model and do you believe it to be helpful?

Part IV

Ethical Dilemmas

A component of productive police work is to always act in an ethical manner. Morals, values, and ethics are a mystery to many. Some common questions regarding ethics are: "How are they acquired?" and "What do they mean?" What is it to do the right thing, act in the right way, and act in an ethical manner? These questions can be answered by applying Immanuel Kant's categorical imperative:

"To always act in such a way that the maxim of my action can and will be made a universal law."

— Immanuel Kant

"Certain qualities are imperative for entry-level police officers, such as honesty, ethics and moral character. Nowicki identifies 12 traits of highly effective police officers: enthusiasm, good communication skills, good judgment, sense of humor, creative, self-motivated, knows the job and the system, self-confidence, courage, understand discretion, tenacious, and have a thirst for knowledge." (Nowicki, 1999, pp. 45–46)

Physical Aggression and Verbal Abuse

Issue 12

Scenario 37: Lessons with Punch

I was hit, I was pushed, I was shoved, he dug his knee into my back, he twisted my arm until it was black, he punched me in the face, he sprayed my body with mace, he kicked me twice, he beat me with his ASP, I cried. He banged my head into the car, he tightened the cuffs where blood ran far, he blackened my body, he spit in my eye, she held me while he screamed, "You're mine now sucker!" I wanted to die!

"The officers at the scene exercised excessive force in order to secure the compliance of the driver, Rodney King. However, much to the chagrin of the officers, George Holliday was able to capture the incident on tape. King was repeatedly beaten by several police officers." (1991)

"Abner Louima was arrested during a fight outside of a New York nightclub. He was taken to the 70th precinct. Officer Volpe sodomized Louima with a broom stick." (1997)

Scenario 38: Irritation

I was chased down the street for walking on some old guy's grass. An officer who hit me with his ASP and shoved me to the ground caught me. He would not allow me to get up until I promised that I would never walk on that old man's grass again.

Scenario 39: Um Good

I was arrested for public intoxication. I was thrown onto the street and handcuffed as my face was buried in the gravel. I could not breathe because I had a mouth full of dirt and gravel. The officer made me swallow it.

Scenario 40: We Got Your Number

I was fighting at a bar, but I did not start it. My girlfriend initiated the fight, and I had to protect her. I was taken to the station, and every officer on duty that night attacked me verbally and physically.

I was on death row for awhile for a crime that I did not commit. I was found innocent and released. However, my name was muddied, and they knew it. They called me scumbag, gang banger, and told me to stay out of their town. They spit on me in the station, kept pushing my head against the wall, and ultimately held me for two days with no charges.

Scenario 41: The Bully

My friends and I are underage but always buy beer and cigarettes. This one cop tracks us down every Friday night. He throws me out of the way and steals our cigarettes and beer. He calls me a loser and dirtball in front of all my friends. He grabs my hand and squeezes it until I begin to cry in front of my friends, then he punches me one last time and leaves the scene.

Today, police brutality and verbal abuse are not acceptable law enforcement practices. Police officers have a tendency to be fashionably rough. Mainly, the academy is responsible for this practice because a fear factor is highlighted when teaching arrest tactics. Many times an officer could walk into a situation and lose his or her life. An officer does not want to be injured, therefore is taught to approach a situation with aggressive behavior. However, in certain instances, this behavior can escalate once one becomes caught up in the moment. An adrenalin rush becomes overwhelming, and a surge of aggression may take control of the officer's mind, overriding professionalism. A professional officer will refrain from verbal abuse and/or physical aggression. Moreover, an officer will practice methods that will maintain control over one's physical being. Falling captive to subconscious and experiencing an intense urge to punish by means of force and abuse are not accepted law enforcement practices. Close and Meier (1995) identify in Carl B. Klockars *Blue Lies and Police Placebos* the ends of force: "*The domination and control [that] force seeks is physical*" (p. 229).

As one is aware, the courts are responsible for punishment. Pollock (1998) explains why police use force in an attempt to punish: *"For instance, police may feel that use of force in some situations results in quick justice that the courts are unable to deliver"* (p. 150).

Officers have the ability to use force, and sometimes that capability is abused. Furthermore, when the use of force is abused and publicized, its negative effect is reinforced to the public. Kerstetter (1985) says:

[T]he appropriate use of coercive force is the central problem of contemporary police misconduct. Indeed we would go further, to argue that the history of policing has been characterized by a dynamic search for the means by which to optimize the use of legitimate force: utilizing it as necessary to maintain order, but not to the extent that it is excessive and abusive. (p. 149)

The term *force* naturally provokes fear, which correlates with a negative public perception. Dempsey (1999) is concerned with the negative public perception of law enforcement. *"Nothing undermines public confidence in the police and in the process of criminal justice more than the illegal acts of police officers"* (p. 296).

Furthermore, police brutality has devastated citizen–officer relations.

Verbal abuse is not an uncommon practice. Derogatory terms can be linked to the us versus them mentality. Walker (1992) identifies this tendency:

Derogatory terms are often an expression of the general alienation of police officers from the public. In specific situations, officers use them as a control technique: to establish their authority by humiliating or demeaning the citizen. (p. 234)

Racial slurs, insulting language, threatening language, and overall curtness are routinely practiced by law enforcement officials. Walker (1992) said:

Observations of police at work have found that offensive labels for people are a regular part of the working language of police officers. Reiss found that 75% of all the officers observed used some racially offensive terms. (p. 234)

A professional officer will employ genuine communication methods, which will create genuine productivity, control situations, alleviate tension, and establish positive outcomes.

Verbal abuse is more prevalent than physical abuse. Dempsey (1999) suggests an advancement of verbal abuse: *"Despite the high incidence of headlines about police brutality, evidence suggests that the verbal abuse of citizens by officers is a more serious problem."*

Dempsey (1999) also took note of a study conducted by Albert J. Reiss Jr. relative to police abuse. The study identified the most common complaints about police officers: "*Use of profane and abusive language, use of commands, stop and frisk violations, threatening force, brandishing a night stick or pistol, and use of physical force*" (p. 303).

A professional officer will not employ verbal or physical abuse in any situation.

Assignment Guide Issue 12: Physical Aggression and Verbal Abuse

Group discussion assignment

- Read Scenario 37 aloud and discuss. What are the adverse effects of this behavior?

- Read Scenario 41 aloud and discuss. What changes have you seen in police brutality over the past several years? Do you believe it's on the decline or are we witnessing even more events? Why or why not?

Corruption

Issue 13

Scenario 42: Overall Theft

Wallets, money, lighters, cigarettes, knives, pocket change, fireworks, bottles of booze, and all small collectibles are confiscated by police officers every day. Subsequently and, supposedly, put into lock-up. Where? Do we have a room for that stuff? Oh, I didn't know.

Scenario 43: It's All About Me, Man!

Kickbacks, bribes, favors, gratuities, theft, Fourth Amendment violations, shake-downs, smack-downs, and abusive crack-downs—all in pursuit of personal gain epitomizing corruption. Hey man, count me in!

Scenario 44: No One Will Know

It was a routine search warrant. I was present along with three other officers. Another officer and I entered the premises and began our search. I noticed an open safe in the wall. We opened the safe and found $25,000 cash inside. I went to get a baggy to put the money in, and when I returned the money was gone. When I asked the other officer about it, he claimed that he never saw any money. He repeated this claim several times in front of the other officers. I knew that he took the money.

Scenario 45: Boom Boom!

It was the night of the fireworks show. As a rookie officer, I observed and stood guard on the outer perimeter of the display. At the end of the night my lieutenant called me over to his vehicle. He opened his trunk and said, "Surprise!" There must have been 5,000 different fireworks in his trunk. He told me to pick one, anything I wanted. Of course, I did.

Scenario 46: Sneaky

We made a routine arrest on a Friday night. When my field-training officer frisked the individual, he found two knives, one switchblade, and a lighter. He put all four items into his pocket, and we never spoke of it again.

Scenario 47: The Categorical Imperative

You are chasing two subjects who have just stolen a pair of sunglasses from a department store and have already run one mile. You are becoming angrier and angrier because you are tired. You become frustrated, weak, and disgusted. Finally you catch up to the petty offenders. They are laughing at you! Did you decide to strike one of them? Grab one of them and throw the subject forcefully to the ground? Maybe elbow one of them in the nose? Hopefully if you chose the latter, it wasn't caught on tape! I got it! Charge the subjects with a felony rather than a misdemeanor. In fact, the crime no longer regards one pair of sunglasses worth $100; it now will involve a factional $1,000 worth of merchandise. That will teach them to steal, making me run two miles.

One must recall the imperative and consider the situation. The subjects were probably scared. They might have been scared of what you might do to them. They might be thinking about the forthcoming wrath of their parents. It's possible that they never intended to steal. In fact, it might have been a dare, juveniles love dares. Put yourself in their position; how would you want to be treated by the police if you were in this situation? More importantly, however, your correct reaction can and should be made a universal law.

Corruption in law enforcement still exists. Whether stealing on a search warrant, frisking a subject and taking personal items, searching a vehicle without probable cause, accepting gratuities in exchange for favors, or routinely shaking down juveniles for packs of cigarettes, corruption surrounding officers is widespread. Corruption can be rectified by an applicable moral philosophy. Morals, values, and ethics can be a personal puzzle. What it is to do the right thing, to act in the right way, and to decide what is good versus what is bad? These are difficult questions to answer. Immanuel Kant's categorical imperative will aid in answering these questions: *"To always act in such a way that the maxim of my action can and will be made a universal law."*

Having ethics means having a set of moral principles. It's time to critically analyze what is right and what is wrong. By following Kant's categorical imperative, one should be aware of what is right and what is wrong. First, clarification of Kant's philosophy is needed. In addition to following Kant's imperative, background information for evaluation purposes is necessary. He believes that human beings have a duty to act in a right way and to act in a right way toward other human beings. Furthermore, human life is the pinnacle of intrinsic worth.

Immanuel Kant regards human life as an end and not as a means to an end. In contemporary society we continuously use individuals as a means to an end. Sometimes we have good reason to do so. For instance, when a subject is interrogated concerning information relating to a crime or in regard to relinquishing information about another individual, the subject is being used as a means to an end. The means-to-an-end philosophy also concerns utilitarianism: the greatest good for the greatest number principle, which Kant strongly opposes. If, for instance, a plane carrying 200 people is overtaken by terrorists who redirect its path to crash into the Sears Tower, but the United States government shoots it down first, this concept would relate to using the individuals on the plane as a means to an end and the greatest good for the greatest number principle is achieved. The means were that the 200 lives on the plane were sacrificed and the end is that we saved 2,000 individuals from death by preventing the targeted crash. In sum, the greatest good for the greatest number principal was a success.

The categorical imperative incorporates an implied conformity rule. If the action should be made a universal law, subsequent conformity is demanded. Kant's categorical imperative can be used as an algorithm and, if followed, can clarify instances of uncertainty in that an established method for determining ethical certainty may be secured. *"If I claimed revenge by brutally beating suspects, would I want that practice to be made a universal law?" "If I become a corrupt law enforcement officer, would I want every officer to follow suit?" "If I stole on search warrants, would I want everyone to be a thief?" "If I sexually harassed someone, would I want everyone to act that way?" "If I searched vehicles with no probable cause, would I want that practice to be a universal law?"* Of course not, because it might happen to you. A set of ethical and good conduct standards personally relating to the professional officer are in need. One must have a disciplined philosophy to apply in times of uncertainty. More important, ability to act subsequent to application should be routinely emphasized. If we as law enforcement officials constantly remind ourselves of the categorical imperative, we will become better human beings and better law enforcement officers.

Assignment Guide Issue 13: Corruption

Group discussion assignment

- Discuss different types of corruption. Read scenarios 42–47. What can we do to change this type behavior?

- Do you believe in-service training to be an option? Why or why not?

Gratuities

Issue 14

Scenario 48: Great Dog Gratuity

Barney at Red Hot Dogs gives you a free lunch every day, and you graciously accept the lunch and thank Barney. It is Friday night when a call comes in from Barney's home; it is a domestic call from his wife. She claims that Barney attacked her, blackened her eye, and pushed her down the stairs. You think to yourself, "Every day for two years, I've received a free lunch from Barney's restaurant. Barney has become my good friend."

Scenario 49: The Favor

You routinely stop at the neighborhood convenience store where all uniformed officers drink free. The owner, Jay, has become your good friend. In fact, you talk with him about an hour every night while you drink your free Pepsi and eat a few free doughnuts. One night Jay asks you for a favor. He tells you about a civil problem he has with an old friend. He bought a motorcycle from this guy a year ago, but the guy never gave him the title. He needs the title fast because he wants to sell the bike. He wants you to go to the old friend's house in uniform, retrieve the title, and scare him a bit. You explain to Jay that this is a civil matter now, it is not in your scope of duty, and that you would need a warrant to go into the guy's house and take papers. Jay does not care about your excuses, and he reminds you of your free food and drink that you have taken every night for a year. He emphasizes that he really needs this favor!

Scenario 50: Lock and Load

Working as a police officer demands that you spend time at the range. Firearm qualification and practice are required. The range master becomes your friend. In fact, he does not even charge you for range time anymore. When you run out of agency ammunition, he offers you free ammunition. You take it and have a blast. One Saturday afternoon, you are indulged in semi-rapid-fire when you notice your friend, the range master, teaching his children and their friends how to shoot a 9mm. Sig Sauer and .357 Smith & Wesson.

He motions for you to come over and asks if you, a police officer, will teach his oldest daughter, who is 17, how to shoot. The state that you live in requires one to be of a certain age and possess a license to discharge a firearm.

Scenario 51: Beef and Cheddar

The local fast food joint gives free beef and cheddars to all on-duty officers. When one is in uniform, the local fast food joint is the place to be. While you are eating your dinner, the manager screams at an employee and throws a cup of ice, which hits the employee in the face. She asks you what you are going to do about this.

Scenario 52: Nickels and Dimes Investigator Frenzy

You are working as a private investigator for a licensed company. Your next-door neighbor sends over food about four times a week. You befriend your neighbor. Even though you tell her not to send over food, you eagerly await the meals and you are eating great. She asks for a favor. Her sister believes that her husband is unfaithful, and your neighbor asks you to independently investigate. However, you must be licensed in the state you reside in to practice independently. You tell your neighbor that for liability reasons you must work through your company. You provide her with information on how to contact your company to initiate the investigation. Your neighbor insists that she does not want to go through your company and offers to slip you money on the side for your work. You inform your neighbor that you cannot help her. She telephones you the next day and asks if she were to call your company and request you to investigate, would you only bill the company for one hour of work and any other time you spend she will pay you under the table?

There are ethical concerns relating to the acceptance of gratuities. *Gratuity* means acceptance of a favor in exchange for some type of act. However, a police officer at the time he or she is accepting this gratuity does not identify with consequences of the gratuity. Gratuities in any form—liquor, magazines, candy, soda, coffee, food, money, discounts, and gifts—are easily offered and easily accepted. If an officer is doing a job as everyone else on a routine daily basis, then why is the officer offered benefits? Miller and Hess (2002) identify the inequality and code of silence practiced by law enforcement.

A belief that officers are above the law, coupled with the code of silence previously discussed can leave officers in ethical dilemmas. A study by the National Institute of Justice, The Measurement of Police Integrity, surveyed 3,235 officers from 30 departments and found that the majority of respondents would not report a fellow officer for accepting gifts, meals or discounts, or for having a minor traffic accident while under the influence of alcohol. (p. 47)

A professional officer will exemplify a zero-tolerance policy on accepting gratuities. The categorical imperative would forbid acceptance of free lunches because if everyone did, capitalism would not exist and Barney would be out of business. Instead, the officer has chosen to accept the food and now feels a duty toward Barney. A bias and a communication filter become apparent. Therefore, Barney's situation may be handled differently than a similar situation. Ethics and morals in policing are spoken and written about, and a formal manual of standards is handed out. However, the way to apply the standards has not been prescribed. Learning how to respond to unethical situations and how to apply an ethical standard will be an easy task if the categorical imperative becomes principle.

Assignment Guide Issue 14: Gratuities

Group discussion assignment

- Please read Scenario 48 and discuss the complications of this situation.
- While on the job, is it OK to accept a simple cup of coffee? Why or why not?

Fourth Amendment Violations

Issue 15

"The right of the people to be secure in their persons, houses, papers, and effects, against unreasonable searches and seizures, shall not be violated, and no warrants shall issue but upon probable cause, supported by oath or affirmation, and particularly describing the place to be searched, and the persons or things to be seized."

— Fourth Amendment to the United States Constitution

Scenario 53: I Was Ready This Time

Every time I get pulled over, an officer tells me to get out of the car and searches my vehicle. This time I was ready. I arrived home late from school. I live in a semi-bad area so I wanted to park my car across the street in another parking lot. I parked my car and got out of my car when I heard a voice say, "Get over here." There was a police car, and sitting in it was a police officer. He asked me to go get my license and bring it to his car. I did. He looked at my license and then looked at me and said, "I am going to search your car now." Luckily, I had just left class and our topic was privacy, highlighting Fourth Amendment violations. I looked him in the eye and said, "Officer, there is no need for that. What probable cause do you have?" He replied, "You're right. Have a good night." He sped away! I never knew what probable cause was. I shared my experience with the class the next week. Thanks, Teach!

Scenario 54: Probable Cause, Duh

"Shawnee Davis, an Olympic speed skater now represented by the NAACP, is suing the Chicago Police Department for an illegal search of his vehicle." (NBC News, March 24, 2003) *Beck v. Ohio*, 1964: "The officer testified that he heard that Beck had a bad reputation, was a gambler, and memorized his appearance. Beck was arrested and searched. Rumors regarding reputation do not constitute probable cause."

Scenario 55: Privacy Not Illegal Embarrassment

I pulled into a dark alley and parked my car. My girlfriend and I wanted some privacy. Along came the police. They demanded that we both get out of the car, and they searched the car as we stood on the side of the road. They opened the glove box and took a pack of gum, my cigarettes, and a pen-like flashlight and then made me open my trunk.

There are many stories of Fourth Amendment violations. The media highlights Fourth Amendment violations, and most citizens do not understand that probable cause is a required element to search a vehicle. A warrant needs to be obtained to search a place, and a full search of a person is only valid if a suspect is arrested. A professional officer is aware that an illegal search and subsequent seizure of evidence can derail an entire case. Furthermore, an illegal search can result in civil liability, criminal prosecution, and enhance the negative perception of law enforcement that persists in society. A professional officer will justifiably and cautiously conduct a search of a vehicle only when probable cause exists (*Carroll v. United States,* 1925), consent is given (*Schneckloth v. Bustamonte,* 1973), or an arrest is made (*Washington v. Chrisman,* 1982).

To react to probable cause, a belief must be substantiated by facts that a crime has been committed, a crime is in progress, or a person has been arrested. Mere suspicion is unwarranted, evidence is in demand, and generally notable only in the case of arrest. Siegel (1997) defines probable cause.

Probable cause to search a place and seize evidence consists of facts that would lead a prudent person to believe that items sought are siezable items (i.e., contraband, the fruits of a crime, instrumentalities used to commit a crime, or evidence of criminality) that are or soon will be located at a particular place. (p. 197)

However, high-profile exceptions to probable cause exist (there are other exceptions to probable cause, which we do not highlight). These high-profile exceptions are: plain view (*Harris v. United States, Arizona v. Hicks,* 1987), open field (*Oliver v. United States,* 1984), and consent to search.

> Plain view: If a vehicle is pulled over for speeding and a firearm or drugs, for instance, are on the front seat of the vehicle in plain view of the officer, a search can be initiated.

> Open field: If a plane is flying over an open field and drugs are seen being produced, a search can be conducted.

> Consent: If an officer asks an individual if he or she can conduct a search and the individual gives consent, then a search can be conducted.

A professional officer is aware that a traffic ticket does not justify probable cause to search a vehicle, and that a warrant is required upon entrance to a home. Entering a home without a search warrant will result in exclusion of evidence collected from the home for trial (*Boyd v. United States,* 1886; *Weeks v. United States,* 1914; *Mapp v. Ohio,* 1961). We refer to this as the exclusionary rule, which was thought to have been a deterrent for police officers. Justice Harry Blackmun reviewed the Oaks research and other studies conducted on the deterrent effect and decided that there is *"no conclusive evidence that the rule has or does not have a deterrent effect.* The *fruits of the poisonous tree doctrine* (*Silverthorne Lumber Co. v. United States,* 1920, exclusionary rule) *becomes a cost/benefit procedure for police officers."* If beneficial means can be produced from violating an individual's Fourth Amendment rights, for instance, the end result being that the evidence might be included in court rather than excluded, an officer ponders; is the illegal risk worth taking? After an officer consistently applies the categorical imperative to situations, he or she will avoid illegal practices. Critical reasoning by an officer pursuing ethical standards before acting illegally should be practiced routinely, respectfully, and considered the goal of genuine police work.

Assignment Guide Issue 15: Fourth Amendment Violations

Group discussion assignment

- What does the Fourth Amendment state?
- What is probable cause?
- Discuss examples and exclusions to the rule of probable cause.

Lying and Policing an Accepted Practice

Issue 16

Scenario 56: The Cabana Boy

I was living in my parent's cabana in the back yard. At about 7:30 a.m., I heard pounding on my cabana door. It was the police. They told me to get out and that they were going to search the cabana. I did not know that they could not search my cabana without a search warrant. I told them that I did not want them to search the cabana. They stated that without a warrant they could search not only the cabana, but my parents' house, too. They did not have a search warrant. Lesson learned.

Scenario 57: But My Parents

I was told that if I gave up the name of my friend I would get to go home. The officers kept repeating, "Just tell us everything that happened and you won't get in trouble."

Scenario 58: Huh, Immunity?

"If you turn in all your drug connections, we will see to it that you receive immunity." They promised me, so I cooperated. Then, after I gave them all the names they needed, an officer said, "Welcome to your new life as a prisoner!"

Scenario 59: Subject Preparation

I work for the railroad. I was caught stealing items from the cars when they arrived at the station. I knew that I was wrong for doing it and I felt terrible. When the officers questioned me, I was cooperative. In fact, the one officer simply told me to do the right thing, so I did. The supervising officer yelled at me, threatening that if I was not cooperative I would go to jail, but if I was, I would not go to jail. I had already decided to cooperate and do the right thing. Finally, I asked if I returned the merchandise, would

I get to keep my job? The one officer said to do the right thing and that she was not sure about me keeping my job. I decided to give back the items that I stole anyway. However, the supervising officer kept repeating, "Fine. Don't worry, you can keep your job." Immediately I was fired.

Lying in policing is a generally accepted practice by law enforcement officials, courts, and society. The lies told in the process of conducting a criminal investigation and questioning suspects are two common situations in which the immorality of lying is negated. Most commonly, lying occurs when attempting to obtain confessions. All with the goal of obtaining justice.

However, a dichotomy must be recognized, acknowledging the difference in police duties. An undercover officer has no choice but to lie. An undercover officer might have to pretend to be someone that he or she is not, and therefore, lying becomes a necessity. More important, for the officer it becomes a safety issue. Differentiation of an undercover officer and a uniformed officer must be established. A uniformed officer has no reason to pursue deceit. We focus in this segment on the uniformed police officer.

A uniformed officer's deceitful tactics should be limited. A uniformed police officer lies so that a rapid effect can be established. For instance, in the cabana scenario, the police did not want to put forth the required effort to obtain a search warrant. Therefore, they decided to take advantage of a naive suspect and, in turn, achieved a timely effect. In the case of questioning suspects, whereby fraudulent promises are agreed on; again, less effort is noted because more information is relinquished quickly. Klockars (1984) examines Blue Lies in policing: *"Thus, in the police officer's view, to lie when one can achieve the same effect more efficiently and with less effort is not immoral but stupid"* (p. 531).

However, this practice should change. Professional uniformed officers will rely on the art of communication and persuasion rather than justifying lying, applied for the sake of an immediate end. In addition, during the interrogation process, instead of threatening a subject with jail time, why not explain behaviorally that doing the right thing is important? Coercion and persuasion should take precedence over scare tactics and lying. Explaining to the suspect his or her rights, obligations, and consequences should be the agenda, not making threats or false promises. Individuals who have had negative experiences with law enforcement officials have been lied to at one time or another and/or have taken note of trickery and verbally abusive tactics. A proper interrogation can produce unlimited amounts of information by simply proposing a cost/benefit profile highlighting character benefits rather than acting with fraudulent and/or abusive intent. A professional officer will obtain a search warrant prior to entering a home; will not search a vehicle without probable cause; will not use fraud or verbal threats as an ally, but will employ honest communication that, in turn, will achieve successful and fruitful outcomes while bolstering citizen trust.

Assignment Guide Issue 16: Lying and Policing an Accepted Practice

Group discussion assignment

- In your opinion is it okay for police to lie in order to seek justice? Why or why not?

- Read Scenario 58 and discuss. Was it okay for the officer to lie here? Why or why not?

- How can officers gain information without making misrepresentions to subjects? Role play and give an example of how this might work.

Stop and Frisk

Issue 17

Scenario 60: What the Heck?

Every time I walk down the street, this officer stops me, pats me down, and then insists that I come with him to his squad car where he questions me for an hour. I am a law-abiding citizen.

Scenario 61: Casual Conversation

My friends and I always stand on the corner talking. Every night the same officer shakes us down. We even have to take everything out of our pockets and purses. He takes money and anything of value. We are not doing anything wrong, we are just talking.

Scenario 62: Engagement Party

I went out late one night to a jewelry store. I was planning to ask my girlfriend to marry me. I was looking through the window of the jewelry store at the wedding rings. I had to go out late because we both work days and I had to wait until she was asleep. I spotted the perfect ring, when all of a sudden I heard a voice say, "Don't move." A police officer was standing behind me. I attempted to explain that I was looking for a wedding ring, but he did not listen. He searched my person and walked me back to my car and searched my car, too. Don't we have any privacy?

Scenario 63: *Graham v. Conner* (1989)

Graham, a diabetic, was having a sugar attack. He asked his friend to drive him to the store for some orange juice. When he arrived at the store he felt that the line was too long. So he ran out of the store to go to another store, hoping for a shorter line. Officer Conner saw Graham speedily leave the store and followed. Officer Conner decided to make an investigatory stop. Graham's friend told Officer Conner that Graham was suffering from a diabetic attack. Officer Conner called for backup when Graham fell to the ground. Backup arrived, and one officer handcuffed Graham while ignoring the friend's statements that Graham was sick. The officers carried Graham over to the squad car and placed him face down on the hood of the car. Graham asked the officer to check his wallet for his diabetic card. The officer told him to shut up. Graham suffered a broken foot, a bruised forehead, wrist injuries, shoulder injuries, and a permanent loud ringing in his ear. The court ruled that the officers did not use excessive force during this investigative stop. (U.S.C. [1983])

The stop-and-frisk law arose during the case of *Terry v. Ohio* (1968). Police officers historically and routinely stopped and frisked individuals. Contemporarily, police departments warn officers to limit this exercise because of liability. A *Terry* stop can become a dangerous game. If an officer abuses *Terry*, a series of consequences can follow. Violating any portion of the *Terry* doctrine can result in criminal, civil, and disciplinary action. Today's police officers use discretion when initiating a *Terry* stop. *Terry* is at times being used as a scapegoat, resulting in intrusions into privacy, violating the Fourth Amendment. A professional officer will be aware of the standards involved and act accordingly. *Reasonable suspicion* is only a vaguely defined term, but has justified police officers' actions in stopping a person. Reasonable suspicion can lead to a *Terry* stop and frisk. Reasonable suspicion justifies a brief stop of a suspect for identification questioning and a pat-down. A brief stop is key to completing *Terry* successfully (*United States v. Sharpe* [1985]). In scenario 60, the officer did not act briefly. A safe *Terry* stop would be indicative of an officer noticing or obtaining information via hearsay (extended *Adams v. Williams* [1972]) of a bulge in the suspect's pants and stopping the suspect for a brief pat down, and/or as extended in *Adams*, the officer may reach into the clothing of a suspect when seeking a weapon. The *Terry* rule has been extended to anonymous tips (*Alabama v. White* [1990]).

The courts have clarified a structure for reasonable suspicion in *United States v. Cortez* (1981). The totality of the circumstances must be taken into account. The totality of the circumstances must in all cases contain two focuses: (1) There must be probabilities derived from information regarding a person; (2) The suspicion must involve the assumption that the individual being stopped is involved in wrongdoing. Thus both aspects must be present before reasonable suspicion is founded.

Many extensions of the *Terry* rule have surfaced. The *Terry* doctrine is vague and risky. An officer should have a clear understanding of the limits to *Terry* and react accordingly. A professional officer will become informed on all applicable extensions of *Terry* before exercising it, and always pursuing *Terry* with ethical regard.

Assignment Guide Issue 17: Stop and Frisk

Group discussion assignment

- Examine the case of *Terry v. Ohio* (1968).

- Read Scenario 62. Was there an error on the side of the police? Why or why not?

- Read Scenario 63. What did the court state? Do you agree with this ruling? Why or why not?

Inappropriate Discretion

Issue 18

Scenario 64: Happy Birthday

It was my 21st birthday. It also was my golden birthday. My friends and I were out drinking all night. We left the bar with a bottle of champagne in the car, and the radio was cranked up high. I was driving. I remember flashing lights behind us. I pulled into a parking lot. The officer approached the vehicle and asked me to step out of the car. He issued a sobriety test. I was having a good time performing it! I asked him, "If I give you a kiss will you let me off?" We drove home drunk that night, and I never received a DUI. It was a great birthday.

Scenario 65: Puppies for Sale

My husband and I decided to breed our dog to get a litter of puppies. English Mastiffs are rare dogs, and at the time everyone wanted one. After the puppies were born, my husband took six weeks off of work to care for the newborns, because I was a student and had to attend classes. We interviewed several potential canine caregivers, and then we made our final decision. A police officer really wanted a puppy for his fiancée. I was hesitant in selling puppies to unmarried couples for stability reasons. I set my concerns aside and sold the puppy to the officer. I stipulated in writing that no returns would be honored. Three months later the officer called, wanted to return the puppy, and wanted his money back. His fiancée and he had broken up.

I had discussed the terms with this officer, and he knew that I was a student in the town that he patrolled. I refused to give him his money back. Every night thereafter when I attended school, I received a parking ticket. I had been given 25 tickets by the time I gave in and took the puppy back.

Scenario 66: I'm a Cop

I know because I am a police officer that I will never receive a speeding ticket. For that matter, I will never receive any type of ticket. In fact, I was caught spying on my ex-girlfriend, but the cops who caught me at the scene knew that I was a cop, and therefore, nothing ever happened to me. Hey, we take care of our own.

Scenario 67: Blow Horn

My friend and I were driving by a police officer who had a car pulled off to the side of the road. I had a blow horn, and as we drove by the officer, I blew the horn at him. Shortly thereafter, we were pulled over by this same officer who cited us for four violations and continued to repeat, "Let me find another one."

Discretion is a vital law enforcement tool. However, discretion must be used ethically. In instances that involve corruption, gratuities, and bribes, officers tend to lose sight of genuine discretionary techniques. The officer has the means to choose alternatives and determine outcomes. These processes must contain an ethical element; otherwise, discretion can become an avenue toward unlawful events.

Since the age of the *Bobbies*, Police officers have always had to exercise discretion. Regardless of the limitations that administration attempts to implement, discretion still is an active part of the profession. An officer's ethical qualities will determine ethical use of discretion or unethical use of it. Discretion is needed in law enforcement. The application of discretion falls victim to unethical behavior. For instance, the birthday scenario is unethical because the officer accepted a promiscuous act in return for not issuing a citation. Either preference or gratuity can affect an officer's discretion. Showing preferences or accepting gratuities is unethical. Wrobleski and Hess (2003) examine preferences correlated with use of police discretion: *"Some male traffic officers, for example, are known to issue warnings to females who violate laws and to issue tickets to males for the same violation"* (p. 334).

Allowing officers discretion gives them the power to employ unethical discretion. Many types of filters can poison ethical discretion, such as discrimination, prejudice, gender, bribes, stereotyping, racism, and bias. Pollock (1998) determines that discretion can create unethical instances:

However, this opens the door for unethical decisions. The power to make a decision regarding arrest creates the power to make that decision using unethical criteria, such as a bribe in return for not arresting. (p. 152)

The officer must always observe genuine ethics when applying discretion in situations. The categorical imperative would not have permitted a kiss in exchange for not being ticketed because sexual gratuities in exchange for freedom would not make for a genuine universal law.

In the puppy scenario, an officer carried out a reprisal against the individual and, therefore, abused his ticket-writing discretion. The officer felt that he was above the law and made it clear that challenging him would result in reprisal, in this case, harassment by issuing parking tickets. Police officers are given a packet of tickets in the expectation that they will be used appropriately and not abused. This constitutes discretion. Abusing ticket-writing privileges simply because an officer has the means to do so, or using the ticket as a coercive tool to gain cooperation or extract a payback or bribe, is unethical. The categorical imperative would not warrant ticket writing as a tool in exchange for a desired end. This would not make for a genuine universal law.

Overall, discretion allows an officer to not issue a ticket, not make an arrest, not to charge someone, not write a biased report, or to determine guilt or to allow a suspect to leave without being charged. An officer on a daily basis decides the fate of individuals and can employ or abuse discretion. Furthermore, if the suspect is a law enforcement officer, then often no violation is issued because, in the mind of the officer, he or she expects like treatment in return. Ethics in discretion can keep an officer honest or lead him or her into ethical dilemmas. The categorical imperative applied to discretion can save an officer from liability, shame, and criminal action.

Scenario 68: Leads Computer

> When I was 18 years old, I was living in a city well known for gang-violence. I had a lot of friends who were connected to gangs, although I was never in one. My friends and I were driving to the store one day when we were pulled over by the police. The officer took my name and date of birth. Today I am 27 years old and was pulled over just last week. The officer screamed for me to exit my car, lie on the ground, and put my hands behind my back. When the officer approached me, he picked me up and threw me against my car. I was in shock. I found out that I was listed in the Leads computer from nine years ago and it read: Gang Relations. How do I get that off my record?

In almost every squad car, officers have access to suspect/offender records through computerized Leads. However, there is only one issue that an officer has the personal power to input into the Leads computer, and that is *Gang Relations*. Once an officer inputs *Gang Relations* under a suspect's or offender's name, it is permanent unless at a later date the officer who entered it personally removes it. The officer in question should have been certain that the suspect was a gang member before inputting such a remark. The Leads System should not allow any officer to input information because it is permanent and can be used as a form of bias, retaliation, or inappropriate discretion. A professional officer, when entering such a remark on a suspect's record, subsequently should keep notes on the subject. If the subject matures and no longer is involved in a gang, the departmental records should be re-evaluated and updated every 10 years. The officer needs to take responsibility for removing such a remark.

Assignment Guide Issue 18: Inappropriate Discretion

Group discussion assignment

- Read Scenario 66. If you were the officer stopping the vehicle, what would you have done differently?

- In Scenario 67 do you think the tickets were warranted? Why or why not?

Ticket Quotas

Issue 19

Scenario 69: I Gotta Make My Quotas Tonight

> I was in training, and every night my FTO (Field Training Officer) would remind me that I was on probation. He reminded me that I had to write at least 10 parking violations per night. When I asked my FTO what would happen if I didn't make my quota, he replied, "Oh, they find a way to get rid of you."

The subculture of policing has many internal unwritten rules. For instance, citation quotas regarding moving violations, parking ticket quotas, and arrest quotas are familiar to all law enforcement officers. FTOs highlight ticket quotas as forms of production and promotion, and officers are reviewed accordingly. Questions arise about these requirements such as: What if an officer cannot locate 10 parking violations during his or her shift? What if the officer cannot find one felony arrest during his or her shift? What if the officer cannot make two misdemeanor arrests during the shift? In such situations, ethical dilemmas have a high probability of surfacing. The officer may have to identify innocent suspects and create fictional charges to meet his or her quota. The officer might have to issue illegitimate parking tickets or moving violations. The officer may have to provoke subjects to act unruly so he or she can issue a routine charge such as disorderly conduct. If officers cannot meet a departmental quota, then provoking a suspect into a chargeable offence becomes necessary. Quotas are an instigator of corruption. Police departments should not emphasize officer arrest or citation quotas. Professional FTOs will not enforce quotas on new recruits. A professional officer will issue citations and act on arrests only in legitimate instances.

Assignment Guide Issue 19: Ticket Quotas

Group discussion assignment

- Should an officer be mandated to write tickets every night on the job? Why or why not?

Part V

An Officer's Personal Life: Is It Really Worth It?

Media Criticism

"There is only one success—to be able to spend your life in your own way."

— Christopher Morley

"If a house be divided against itself, that house cannot stand."

— Mark 3:25

Let it be known that what is said about men and women affecting upon their personal and professional lives, and destinations; more importantly, it's affecting upon how they act.

At times a treacherous journey for police officers ends with difficult decisions. Much to the chagrin of officers who were prepared to aid fellow Americans, shockingly they may find themselves justifying their career choice. The effects of the media, job, scrutiny, administrative standards, and shaky domestic lifestyle of an officer all can potentially contribute to an emotionally unsound and confused individual. The media has painted a disturbing picture of law enforcement officials. In fact, television and movies drip with corruption, violence, lack of integrity, and lack of honesty. The media does not take into account generalized effects of its messages, which in turn demand answers from headquarters that weigh heavily on the minds of officers.

The intense scrutiny from the system many times concludes in attempted suicides, aggressive behavior, and/or isolation from the outside world. What the public or the new recruit does not know is that inside the mind of an officer is a conscious world. An officer must live in a pressurized world demanding an embodiment of low profiles, high levels of scrutiny, reaction or no action, a steady hand or a lack thereof, reservation in the presence of their friends/family, an example for society, a perfect record, a perfect credit history, and an all-around picture-perfect life. The pressure relating to his or her personal life begins at training and continues throughout one's law enforcement career. An officer's world is different from many others, quietly catered to, but internally a constant battle. This world can spur emotional trauma, anxiety, and remoteness. The day in the life of an officer is pressure-filled, with constant scrutiny of officer behavior and overall demands of performance excellence. How many jobs examine one's personal life? Can you imagine a job interview for any other position that would evaluate your personal life? A police officer is surrounded by tough decision-making practices, intense scrutiny, stressful circumstances, and, overall, a media focusing on fictionalized, questionable policing. Prior to embracing a vocation in policing, one should critically evaluate the circumstances of such a position.

— K. Karlberg

Scenario 70: Bad Day

Arriving at work, I saw that my supervisor was distraught and unusually quiet. He did not speak to me, so I was at a loss for assignments. The entire day he read the paper, which featured a former corrupt cop from his division who was currently on trial.

Scenario 71: The Movies

The Hurricane, *Training Day*, *Serpico*, *The Bad Lieutenant*, and *Internal Affairs* … Movies portray officers leading lives of corruption and deceit.

Scenario 72: The News

Waco, Ruby Ridge, sniper incidents, Bill of Rights violations, prison beatings, injured suspects, and other police misdeeds are highlighted every night on television.

Scenario 73: The Radio

Pigs, bacon, 5-0 stinks, Poe Poe, shumucks, rats, narks, and fuzz are common terms featured in the media used to describe police officers.

In the eyes of an officer, the media is largely responsible for society's negative perception of law enforcement. The media has portrayed lifestyles of police officers as deceitful and violent. Television, movies, news, radio, online, newspapers, and other forms of communication paint disturbing pictures of law enforcement. Disturbing movies that portray cops as violent and malicious individuals are common. Movies that highlight corruption of officers and radio shows that label officers as *dirty pigs* are featured regularly. An officer must learn how to respond to these criticisms. The average citizen is proud to announce employment status and boast about accomplishments. *How can an officer refer to employment status with confidence?*

Take note that officers portrayed as heroes on television are few and far between. One movie is indicative of a police officer portrayed as a hero: *Colors*. In fact, usually only negative outcomes are documented. For instance, Joseph Maginowski (1991) was sentenced to life in prison. Maginowski was a former Chicago police officer who was tasked to the ATF and who became a corrupt officer. Maginowski's case was continuously broadcast on television, and his face was highlighted on the front page of the papers from the beginning of the incident. A decade later, it still appears on television, radio, and newspapers.

If an officer arrives at work to find an angry supervisor or a quiet supervisor or a lackadaisical supervisor due to negative media exposure of another officer, that officer's day becomes confusing and stressful. An officer is haunted by not wanting to say the wrong thing, acknowledge the wrong issue, or speak about the negative occurrence. Therefore, tip-toeing around negative issues becomes a habit.

At the forefront of dinner conversation or at a family barbeque is an officer's personal life. Due to the fact that the media emphasizes negative occurrences, questions involving the life of an officer from loved ones are a frequent subject of conversation. Explanation is demanded even though the officer being questioned is not the officer under scrutiny. A professional officer will simply highlight the fact that not all law enforcement officers behave in a corrupt fashion, and that the media exaggerates incidents. If the media would highlight the positive accomplishments of law enforcement, that would relieve a lot of stress and allow an officer to be proud of identifying him- or herself as a police officer.

Assignment Guide Issue 20: Media Criticism

Group discussion assignment

- Do you feel officers are treated fairly when featured in the media?

- Do negative media portrayals of officers influence public perception? How?

- Read Scenario 73. Does this type language negatively affect officers? What in your opinion are the long-term effects on officers related subjected to this type of verbal abuse?

Family

Communication

Issue 21

Scenario 74: My Second Wife Is Leaving Me, Too?

When I arrive home, I don't like to speak about my negative day. My vocabulary has turned into street talk. Derogatory terminology has grown on me. I am always yelling, screaming, and using vulgar words. I have been a beat cop for 20 years and am not home on holidays or weekends. Everybody works on holidays, especially New Year's Eve, Halloween, and the Fourth of July, but my wife does not understand. Once again, my wife is leaving me.

A police officer's home life can be very stressful. Family members have a difficult time accepting schedules and holiday workloads. It is important to alert a prospective spouse on the dangers of the position, the time required, and the lack of holiday time that can be spent with loved ones. Communication about the police officer's job demands is critical in maintaining a healthy and stable home life. The loved one needs to be reminded that the job is important, but that the family is even more important. The family member must be understanding of and in accord with the police officer's position at the onset of the relationship; otherwise, they can be in danger of divorce, break-up, or domestic violence. For the police officer, communicating the job requirements and personal needs at the onset of a relationship is essential to a stable home life.

Assignment Guide Issue 21: Family Communication

Group discussion assignment

- Does the job affect an officer's personal life? How?

- Read Scenario 74. Should an officer discuss his or her job and its demands at the beginning of a relationship? Why or why not?

Partner
Communication

Issue 22

Scenario 75: My Partner Sucks!

My partner is obnoxious and rude. He makes me feel like my night will never end. He only speaks of negative issues. My partner never breathes a positive word. Every time I attempt to speak about the positive aspects of policing, his feedback is negative.

Many seasoned officers tend to behave in a highly negative manner. The modern professional officer must learn to maintain positive communications. For the spouse, communicating with your partner on a daily basis sometimes seems trying. Through reinforcing positive communication, an officer can begin to change his or her mindset to a more positive one. Jokes are a positive technique, along with positive stories about home life or job. If a partner tends to dwell on prior negative experiences, attempt to problem solve and identify how the incident could have taken a positive spin. A professional officer employs positive partner communication, and does not dwell on negative experiences.

Assignment Guide Issue 22: Partner Communication

Group discussion assignment

- How important is it for an officer to learn to understand different personalities?
- Read Scenario 75. How would you address this situation?

Negative Energy

Issue 23

Scenario 76: I Need to Get Drunk

I remember one night when I was called to the scene where a suspect had a firearm. I was the acting lieutenant that evening and I was shot at. When I got home, I did not speak to anyone. I sat quietly and drank as much alcohol as I could. I got so smashed that I put my fist through the wall. When I woke up for work the next day, I was hung over, late, and my wife was furious with me.

Police officers need to relieve stress after a long day's work. Negativity of the position is constant, which results in stress for officers. Many effects of police stress result in alcoholism, substance abuse, and sometimes even suicide. This officer might have chosen to jog after work or visit the local gym to exercise. An officer needs stress relievers, such as positive communications with family, counseling, meditation, massage therapy, music, and any other non-chemical means that the officer finds effective. Physical abuse, chemical abuse, and verbal abuse can also be stress relievers, but of the wrong kind. Divorce rates are rising for officers because a common theme of leaving one's work at the office is expected, yet difficult to accomplish. Bringing home concerns of a day's work to an understanding loved one or into a counseling-type setting is a necessity in relieving stress. Emotionally healthy officers on the street and at home maintain a positive persona and focus on positive outcomes and positive energy. Officers must initiate positive changes, opening the floodgates to positive interactions with their family and the community rather than negative ones.

Assignment Guide Issue 23: Negative Energy

Group discussion assignment

- What are some options to relieve job-related stress?
- Is it okay to discuss sensitive issues with your spouse? Why or why not?

Administrative Stress

Issue 24

Scenario 77: The Chain of Command: Now Everybody Knows

Officer Smith, a lieutenant on a different shift, always bothered me. At every meeting he would invade my space by putting his face next to mine while whispering compliments of a sexual nature. I asked him to stop behaving in such a way. He refused and continued to harass me. When I told my sergeant, he told my lieutenant, and a meeting was scheduled with several other officers as witnesses. I ended up being blamed for not being able to accept compliments. Now the entire department is aware of the incident.

The compliments created an uncomfortable work environment for this officer. The sergeant and the lieutenant on the officer's shift should have handled this situation privately. Instead, they alerted the chain of command and other officers of the matter, which resulted in stress for the complaining officer as well as harassment from other officers and embarrassment. A professional supervisor would have handled the matter privately, addressing the incident with each individual separately.

Assignment Guide Issue 24: Administrative Stress

Group discussion assignment

- What is the chain of command?
- What is sexual harassment? Watch the movie *Serpico*.

Badge It: An Everyday Part of Life

Issue 25

Scenario 78: Bars

The cool thing about being a cop is that I can get in to any bar anytime I want without standing in line or paying a cover charge.

Scenario 79: Concerts

My friends and I had tickets to a concert, but they were nosebleed seats. They suggested that I tried "badging it" to move to the front row. I did, we had second row center seats the entire night.

Scenario 80: Anywhere I Go

Anywhere at any time, I can do whatever I want because I simply "badge it"!

Scenario 81: Ticket? Yeah Right!

Hey, every time I get pulled over I wave my badge out the window and wait for the other officer to signal for me to keep going!

One of the perks in the personal life of an officer is carrying a badge. The badge can be used anywhere for entrance into unauthorized areas, free food, and avoiding moving violations or any violations for that matter. The badge is what most prospective officers look forward to receiving. The status of the badge carries a lot of weight in any circumstance. At times a badge is abused by the officer. A citizen might think, *"If I do not allow this officer to sit in the front row, will he or she retaliate against me? On the other hand, if I do allow this officer to sit in the front row, maybe I will not receive any traffic tickets."*

A professional officer does not use the badge in his or her personal life. A professional officer pursues equality at all times and does not use a badge for personal gain. A potential law enforcement recruit will be aware of the negative offerings of this position prior to employment. A potential law enforcement recruit will critically evaluate all aspects of the position, including mental and physical strain prior to committing to employment. One must be cognizant of the negative backlash and high level of scrutiny that comes with the job and be able to mentally and physically endure it.

Assignment Guide Issue 25: Badge It: An Everyday Part of Life

Group discussion assignment

- In your opinion do many officers use their badges for event-related activities?
- Should officers be allowed to do this? Why or why not?
- Read Scenarios 78–81. Is this behavior acceptable or should we punish officers for this type of behavior and how?

References

1. Arrigo, Bruce, *Social justice, criminal justice.* New York: Wadsworth Publishing, 1999.

2. Close, Daryl, & Meier, Nicholas. *Morality in criminal justice.* New York: Wadsworth Publishing, 1995.

3. Dantzker, Mark L. *Understanding today's police.* Upper Saddle River, NJ: Prentice-Hall, Inc., 1995.

4. Dempsey, John S. *An introduction to policing.* New York: Wadsworth Publishing, 1999.

5. Eck, J. E., & Spelman, W. *Problem-solving: Problem-oriented policing in Newport News.* Washington, DC, 1987.

6. Fisher, Roger, Ury, William, & Patton, Bruce. *Getting to Yes: Negotiating agreement without giving in,* 2nd ed. New York: Penguin, 1991.

7. Kant, Immanuel. *The critique of pure reason,* 1781.

8. Kerstetter, W. A. Who disciplines the police? Who should? In W. Geller (Ed.), *Police leadership in America: Crisis and opportunity.* New York: Praeger, 1985.

9. Klockars, Carl B. *Blue lies and police placebos.* Thousand Oaks, CA: Sage Publications, 1984.

10. Lundman, Richard J. *Police and Policing.* New York: Holt, Rinehart and Winston, 1980.

11. Maslow, A. H. A theory of human motivation. *Psychological Review,* 50(1943), 370–396.

12. Miller, L. S., & Hess, K. M. *The police in the community.* New York: Wadsworth Publishing, 2002.

13. Muir, William. Police: *Streetcorner politicians.* Chicago: University of Chicago Press, 1977.

14. O'Brien, Maureen. *Who's got the ball (And other nagging questions about team life).* New York: American Management Association, 1995.

15. Pollock, Jocelyn. *Ethics in crime and justice,* 3rd ed. New York: Wadsworth Publishing, 1998.

16. Reece, Barry L., & Brandt, Rhonda. *Effective human relations,* 8th ed. Houghton Mifflin Co., 2002.

17. Tosi, H. L., Rizzo, J. R., & Carroll, S. J. *Managing organizational behavior.* Cambridge, MA: Ballinger Publishing Co., 1986.

18. Walker, Samuel. *The police in America.* McGraw Hill Inc., 1992.

19. Wrobleski, Henry M., & Hess, Karen M. *Introduction to law enforcement.* Thomson, Wadsworth, 2003.

20. Zernike, Kate. *The hunt for a sniper: A killer's perspective; Son of Sam Killer Talks of Sniper.* New York: *New York Times,* October 22, 2002.

Additional Reading

1. Bowie, G. Lee, Michaels, Meredith W., & Higgins, Kathleen (Eds.). *Thirteen questions in ethics*. Fort Worth: Harcourt Brace Jovanovich, 1992.

2. Clavell, James (Ed.). Sun Tzu *The art of war*. New York: Dell Publishing, 1983.

3. Hall, Lavinia. *Negotiation strategies for mutual gain*. Thousand Oaks, CA: Sage Publications, 1993.

4. Harris, C. E. *Applying moral theories*. New York: Wadsworth Publishing Company, 1997.

5. Johnson, A. Herbert. *History of criminal justice*. Anderson Publishing, 1996.

6. Krasemann, Keith. *Questions for the soul*. Acton, MA: Copley Publishing, 1997.

7. Mansfield, Harvey (Trans.). Niccolò Machiavelli *The prince*. Chicago: University of Chicago Press, 1985.

8. Messner, F. Steven. *Crime and the American dream*. New York: Wadsworth Publishing Co., 1997.

9. More, Harry W. *Behavioral police management*. New York: Macmillan Publishing Co., 1992.

10. Moser, Paul K. *Human knowledge*. New York: Oxford University Press, 1995.

11. Pope, Carl E., Lovell, Rickie D., & Brandl, Steven G. *Voices from the field*. New York: Wadsworth Publishing, 2001.

12. Rosenbaum, D. P., Lurigio, A. J., & Davis, R. C. *The prevention of crime*. New York: Wadsworth Publishing, 1998.

13. Stojkovic, Stan, Kalinich, David, & Klofas, John. *Criminal justice organizations*. New York: Wadsworth, 1998.

14. Velasquez, Manuel. *Business ethics*. Englewood Cliffs, NJ: Prentice Hall, 1982.

15. Walker, Samuel. *Popular justice.* New York: Oxford University Press, 1998.

16. ———. *Sense and nonsense about crime and drugs.* New York: Wadsworth Publishing, 2001